OMG! I'M HAVING A WHITE CHAIR DAY

by Joni Jesme

OMG! I'm Having a WHITE CHAIR DAY!
or When Mouth and Brain take a Vacation
by Joni Jesme

Copyright ©2017 Joni Jesme
All rights reserved.

First Edition ©2018

FSP
FIRST STEPS
PUBLISHING

Published by
First Steps Publishing
PO Box 571
Gleneden Beach, Oregon 97388-0571
FirstStepsPublishing.com

The stories in the book all come from the author's recollections, though they are not written to represent word-for-word transcripts. Rather, the author has retold them in a way that evokes the feeling and meaning of what was said and in all instances, the essence of the story and dialogue is accurate.

While all the stories in this book are true, some names and identifying details have been changed to protect the privacy of the people involved.

No part of this publication may be reproduced or transmitted in any form or by any means, electronic or mechanical, without permission in writing from the Publisher.

Library of Congress Control Number: 2017941175
Genre: Humorous, humor & entertainment, short stories, mid-life, women's fiction

Cover Design by Suzanne Fyhrie Parrott
Illustrations by Yulia Radich

    ISBN - 978-1-937333-44-7 (hbk)
    ISBN - 978-1-937333-58-4 (pbk)
    ISBN - 978-1-937333-46-1 (epub)

10 9 8 7 6 5 4 3 2 1

Printed in the United States

Dedicated to my sons Aaron and Evan.
Thank you for the 'Free Tacos', the Muffin Man,
cats in laundry chutes, the shaved M,
sauerkraut sandwiches, Big Blue,
Snot Bot Booger Brät,
and this journey we have
traveled . . . together.
You inspire me every day, and
I would do it all over again - 40 times.

CONTENTS

ACKNOWLEDGEMENTS 6
FROM HIGH CHAIRS TO WHITE CHAIRS 8
MILESTONE 1 ~ CHILDHOOD 10
MILESTONE 2 ~ PUBERTY 15
MILESTONE 3 ~ DATING 18
MILESTONE 4 - MARRIAGE 22
MILESTONE 5 ~ MOTHERHOOD.......... 23
MILESTONE 6 ~ DATING—*AGAIN* 32
MILESTONE 7 ~ WHERE IS ALL BEGAN 38
#1 - WRONG RAILING.................... 42
#2 – HOW DRY I AM..................... 44
#3 – KEPT IN THE DARK................. 46
#4 – JUST A LITTLE TO THE LEFT 48
#5 - SOUL FOOD........................ 50
#6 – THE DANCING SPRAYER 52
#7 – NOW WHERE DID I PUT THAT?....... 54
#8 – SO JUMPY......................... 56
#9 – WHERE IS SHE GOING? 58
#10 - MAN-TEE-HOSE!................... 60
#11 – HAIR RAISING EXPERIENCE......... 62
#12 - ALARMING........................ 64

#13 – HOW LOW CAN YOU GO? 66
#14 – WHICH VAN IS IT ANYWAY? 68
#15 – SOGGY BABY DOLL 70
#16 – LET'S PUT A LITTLE LIGHT
         ON THE SUBJECT 73
#17 – A PEACEFUL STORM 76
#18 – BALLS, BALLS, AND MORE BALLS 78
#19 – START YOUR ENGINES? 80
#20 – CHEATERS, CHEATERS, EVERYWHERE 82
#21 – WHICH SIDE ARE YOU ON? 85
#22 – SEE YOU AT THE MOVIES! 87
#23 - HOLD WHAT? 89
#24 – LET ME DRIVE! 92
#25 – IT'S PUMPING COLD OUT HERE! 95
#26 – ONE HOT CART! 98
#27 – FIRE AND BRIMSTONE? 101
#28 - I WAS THERE 104
#29 – SAFE, SOUND AND SECURE 106
#30 – SILENT RELIEF 109
#31 - STATE FAIR LOCKOUT 112
#32 - YOU'RE OUT OF HERE! 114
#33 - WHAT DAY? 117
#34 – WHAT'S **YOUR** FAVORITE? 119
#35 – GROCERIES, CHECK! 122
#36 – KNOCK THREE TIMES 125
#37- MINNESOTA NICE 127
#38 - THE SOUND OF CAPPUCCINO? 130
#39 - HOW OLD ARE YOU? 132
#40 NOT ALL ROADS 135
ABOUT THE AUTHOR 139

ACKNOWLEDGEMENTS

I would like to express my gratitude to the many people who saw me through not only this book but in my journey:

Thank you to my friend Brenda Hartman and a grocery isle encounter where you probed the question, "So what are you going to do with those stories you collected?" Your gentle nudging and introduction to Suzanne brought this to fruition and you are appreciated beyond words.

To my assiduous and witty publisher, Suzanne Parrott at First Steps Publishing for your commitment to collaboration and sharing the humor in all of it. Without you this book would never find its way.

My unwavering, unshakable and beautiful dear friend Lynne Barton; because of you, I didn't give up on so many things. You not only know my stories, but you have also lived them with me. And even in the goofiness we share, you inspire me.

Thank you, mom, for your patience during my adolescent mission to straighten my hair, for not laughing when I did some crazy things, for not giving up when I did crazier, for your advice, your faith, for always understanding. Your loving example will last a lifetime.

To my family and friends for their love and support through everything, *Thank you.*

And finally, thank you to those who have entered their White Chair Days and shared stories, either their own or someone else's.

To those who don't see your stories in this book, *they will be in the next!*

FROM HIGH CHAIRS TO WHITE CHAIRS

A funny thing happened on my way to growing older. I came into my *White Chair Days*. One enters your White Chair Days after a comical and sometimes awkward voyage through life's milestones. However, if you can appreciate the humor as you transition from one phase to another, your White Chair Days will defy expectations, and life will be anything but dull.

This curly-headed, freckled-faced gal stumbled her way through many of life's milestones. Not always with grace, many times tripping over my large feet, but nonetheless, earning and appreciating each stage.

Milestone badges aren't displayed as merit patches sewn on a sash proudly worn across our chest. Instead, they covertly arrive in the form of wrinkles, love handles, and the occasional memory lapses, which causes us say the proverbial "Why did I walk into this room? What was I looking for?" and, of course, "Now, where did I leave my keys?" You know what I'm talking about!

The milestone journey starts at birth—a time when innocence and the perception of infinite lifespans dwell unconsciously in our minds. Too soon, we have raced through childhood, and such memories as using a string tied between a loose tooth and an open fridge door are long forgotten. Those recollections merge with adolescence and then fold into adulthood until, before you know it, you've entered the White Chair Days.

MILESTONE 1

As a child, I hated my freckles. Despite *my* intense dislike toward the invading pigments, they did provide a source of amusement—with one incident standing out.

The drive to my grandparent's farm was long. Between the gentle rocking of the car and the soft whispering of tires against the pavement, I soon found myself lulled to sleep. When I awoke, two giggling faces peered down at me, fingers pointing at my face.

Sibling torments are not unheard of, and I have dispensed my fair share. However, being on the receiving end is far less amusing.

"What are you doing?" I asked.

Through suppressed giggles, they replied, "We're trying to *count* your freckles."

As I reflect on the memory, I can appreciate the cliché, "It could've been worse." Imagine if they'd chosen to use a permanent marker and play 'connect the dots!'"

One of my earliest aspirations was to rid myself of these pigmented intruders. After all, it was *my* face, and I decided *who* lived on it. My dad had freckles on his arms, but not on his face, so when I asked how he got rid of them, he joked, "You have to rub dandelions all over your face."

And of course, *I did.*

I grabbed handfuls of the weeds, smashing their yellow flowers against my freckled cheeks, confident that this magical cure would free me from these unwanted trespassers. I just knew each mutilated blossom was erasing my freckles, and soon my face would be free of the undesirable blemishes—just as it should be.

When the last dandelion lay in a crumpled mess on the lawn, I rushed into the house to view my new, spot-free face in the bathroom mirror. Alas, the mirror reflected yellow-stained cheeks, still very full of freckles. I ran to my dad, tears intermingling with the enemy and my colorful skin.

Upon seeing me, he started to laugh, which turned my tears into laughter too. My dad had just taught me a valuable lesson—to have a sense of humor about myself and of life—to love yourself for who you are.

Now, every spring, when the dandelions poke out of the ground, I pick at least one, and rub it on the back of my hand in memory of my dad and laugh at those yellow stains. And yes, I still have freckles on my face. Perhaps I should try rub dandelions on my cheeks again. Not to get rid of my freckles—*they have grown on me*—but to have another laugh despite them.

My mom was brilliant at transforming boxes into the best hideaways. She, along with my sister and me, made amazing playhouses out of cardboard refrigerator containers, complete with a door, windows, and curtains from scraps of fabric. There is something magical about these structures, especially ones made with a parent. It frees the mind and opens the imagination to where anything is possible. In a perfect world, there would be a law requiring everyone, of any age, to spend time in a handmade fortress.

I believe that those forts were the foundation for my ability to think differently, unconventionally, a 'think outside of the box' perspective on life. Mom, I think you and I should pick up some cardboard boxes and have some fun next time we visit!

When I was a little older, we moved to a small town hobby farm across the railroad tracks. I spent many happy barefoot hours outdoors. I hated shoes, I still do, so my dirty bare feet took me on the adventures of finding salamanders, catching chickens, chasing pigs, hissing back at hissing geese, and trying to ride Sugar, our small horse who didn't like to be ridden. He would stop on the side gravel road, lay down, and refuse to go any further...I think he was partially mule.

In the flat farmland behind our home stood a small circle of pine trees that resembled an island oasis. Spending many hours playing in that grove and its pine needle covered floor, we strolled the woods and the fields, for no reason other than to wander and explore. *I wonder if our nature dwelling is still standing.*

My grandparents' farm had a garage filled with numerous things to 'tinker' with—wood, nails, various kinds of tools, and twine. I'd lay awake at night before our visits, wondering what great things I'd create when we got there.

They allowed us to explore and if I wasn't braiding twine ropes for my grandfather, I was finding something else to do. One night, we got to stay with our grandparents while our parents were away. I asked my grandmother if I could make them a cake. She said yes and allowed me to remain in the kitchen to make my *surprise* dessert. I worked very hard, and when I emerged from the kitchen to present my masterpiece, they were gracious enough to exclaim, "Oh, this is soooo good!", even though my cake consisted of one entire loaf of *homemade bread*, layered with peanut butter and jelly, and frosted on the outside with the same!

They had a chicken coop and one *mean* hen that made collecting eggs a challenge to this little girl. Grandma would laugh when she would recount watching me running across the yard, toward the farmhouse, with that hen chasing behind me, pecking at the back of my heels as we raced! If she were still with us, she would laugh at the irony of my recent visit to an urban farm store in the city to start researching how to raise chickens on my own in the backyard. I mean, who can resist a fluffy little chick?

I learned to make homemade buns with Grandma, and later in life, she confided that she'd swapped out my dirt-stained creation with one she'd made. Apparently, despite washing my hands before rolling the dough, my rounded handiwork had a light gray tinge. Dirt was not to be added to my diet that day!

I trailed her in the gardens, fingers stained red from eating more strawberries from her huge strawberry patch than I picked. Fresh peas popped from their shell and into my mouth, and carrots quickly washed off from the water pump before being devoured. Eating straight from the garden remains one of life's great pleasures for me—fresh and raw, and probably consuming a bit of dirt along the way.

That dirt found its way into my heart. Growing my own herbs and vegetables, getting my hands dirty and sharing this gratifying sensory-filled experience with my sons and others, feeds my soul.

MILESTONE BADGE EARNED: CHILDHOOD

MILESTONE 2

One morning, I woke up, and staring back at me in the mirror was a reluctant shiny metal grin. I reached puberty: the awkward, clumsy, self-conscious, graceless time of your life that seems to last an *ETERNITY*. The onomatopoeic word that imitated my feelings toward this phase: PEW-Brrr-Teee.

When I close my eyes, I can remember that girl, who in her reflection saw a mouth full of braces and headgear shining back at her as if some barbed wire fence had been installed to lock down and conceal her smile forever. Everything at that age seemed like it would *never* end.

Also well-hidden were my breasts, which looked like two eggs in a frying pan (or so I was told), and in my lowered expectations, *longed* to fit into at least a size AA bra. In seventh grade, two classmate friends asked me if I had ever taken the pencil test.

"The pencil test?" I asked half-heartedly, somehow dreading the answer. "Yes, the pencil test," they said. "You take a pencil, put it underneath your boob, and if it stays, you have them. If it doesn't, you don't."

I placed the pencil under my egg-sized breast and... My test sent the pencil not only dropping straight and fast to the floor but rolling across the gym locker room floor. Sigh....

No boobs.

Perhaps I should have used glue!

I was a very tall and skinny youth, and remember being told once, "If you drank a bottle of strawberry pop, you'd look like a thermometer!" I begged my mom to support me on a Hershey candy bar diet. I so desperately wanted to put on some weight. Can you imagine? A Hershey candy bar diet now?

My untamed, frizzy curls had claimed their independence and appeared to spring from my head like a dish scouring pad. It was the 1970s, and Farrah Fawcett's feathered hair was becoming the status quo in hairstyles. If not Farrah feathers, then long, flowing straight locks that swung back and forth. My mother went with me from beauty salon to beauty salon, trying to find that "miracle cure" for my curly hair curse, or at that age, what I thought to be a curse. In one salon, the stylist said, "You should come and feel this girl's hair!"

My mom, my wonderful, super champion supporter, did everything she could to help in my quest for straight hair. We tried mayonnaise treatments, hot oil treatments, infrared light treatments, and reverse perms—my hair must have reeked like a deep-fried bad salad! Mom continued to encourage and support me during these desperate attempts, and despite my disbelief, she'd continually tell me *I was beautiful.*

My mother *is* a beautiful woman, not only because of her fortitude to put up with my straight hair obsession but also for restraining her laughter at each adventure. Throughout it all, she reminded me that *I was beautiful.* I was fortunate to have such a wonderful mom.

The modern curling iron became a pseudo-blessing for me. Instead of twirling the hair into a curl, I pulled the iron downward through my mop of hair. No flowing locks, but a bit straighter until the humidity caused those coils to spring forward again!

During my youth, I had my natural mane cut short as a method of taming the wild beast—or, at least, dealing with a smaller one. My hairstyles ranged from an Afro to a weird curling iron hairdo invention. Imagine one *very large*, perfectly smooth curl across the front of my freckled forehead, and the rest of my hair some short version of "Let It Be." I have a picture of that giant curl across my forehead and laugh every time I see it.

While I dreamed of the straight flowing blonde locks sported by the character Julie Barnes from the show *The Mod Squad*, instead my hair resembled that of her partner, Linc. I still joke that I styled my hair by putting a finger into an electrical socket.

So, who was this person in the mirror, and how did I arrive here?

MILESTONE BADGE EARNED: PUBERTY

MILESTONE 3

As the awkwardness of puberty started to fade, the unknown territory of dating knocked at the door. I wasn't ready—not nearly—and I bumbled my way through high school and young adult romance.

Along came Brian. One of my first, more serious, boyfriends. I met him at a community youth group meeting when I was a junior in high school. He attended the community college. He mesmerized me. Tall, a full beard, unlike the high school boys who sported strands of facial hair reminiscent of Shaggy from *Scooby-Doo*. His dark blond hair had a curly wave to it (*this from the girl trying to get rid of her own curls*), and he resembled my youth crush on Gordon Lightfoot, the way he looked on the cover of *Gord's Gold*. Yum… We shared the love of Steely Dan's *Aja* album and agreed it was the greatest collection of songs ever recorded. But the day Brian wore a flannel shirt *I melted*. Yes, a flannel shirt. A flannel shirt still gets to me to this day.

My mom and dad were nervous. Who could blame them? Our three-year age difference was a big maturity gap especially when a gal is still in high school.

But I was smitten. I worked at a fast food restaurant called Hardee's, not far from the high school. One night a coworker (let's call her Cindy) and I were talking about our boyfriends. We started laughing when we found out we were both going out with guys named Brian. The more we talked, the more we laughed at the similarities between our two Brian's…until it hit us. "Hey, we're dating the same guy!"

Instead of getting mad, we decided to have a little fun. Cindy arranged for Brian to pick her up after work for a date, and I would come in on my night off to help execute our strategic sting. He knew we both worked at the same place, so I wasn't surprised during our telephone conversation the night before when he asked my work schedule.

He walked in at the end of her shift, and Cindy came out of the employee area to greet him. I waited only a few moments, and then I walked out and said, "Hi, Brian!"

You should have seen the look on his two-timing face! We were both without a boyfriend after that, but we gained so much more from the experience. While he wasn't the greatest boyfriend in the world, *Aja* is still one of the greatest recordings of all time.

In my early twenties, I dated a young man whose family had immigrated to the US from Greece. Impressed with the Greek culture, I got swept away by his accent.

His friends got a kick out of teaching me Greek words and had me practice sentences as a surprise for my boyfriend. At a potluck gathering, his friends told him "We have been teaching Joni some Greek!"

As proud as a peacock I cleared my throat and started to recite the few sentences I had been taught, and his eyes grew wide. He looked at his friends, and they all burst out laughing. It took me no time at all to realize that they had been teaching me some pretty vulgar sentences! Periodically, just for fun, my boyfriend would look at me and say, "Joni, speak Greek to me," and we would bust up laughing.

My boyfriend's brother had been in a car accident but recovered fully. The family owned a local Greek restaurant in the city and decided to throw a party to celebrate his full recovery. They closed the restaurant for the festivities for their large group of friends and family. I was invited to come early in the morning to help and learn how to make some of the food. They were going to have moussaka, spanakopita, tabbouleh, rice pilaf, baklava, and lamb grilled on a rotary grill.

When we arrived, he took me by the hand and led me to the back of the restaurant to the kitchen. To my surprise, there was a lamb in the back by the sink area, near a floor drain.

"Oh, how cute!" I said, followed by nervous thoughts of, *wait, there is a lamb in the kitchen…*

He then explained that this lamb was for the celebration feast later that night. *Wait, what?*

Before I could bolt…, let's just say there was fresh lamb meat.

My grandparents had a farm, and I grew up knowing the life cycle from farm to table, but this caught me off guard.

I have no desire to be taken by the hand and led to the back of a restaurant…ever again.

MILESTONE BADGE EARNED: DATING

MILESTONE 4

At the age of twenty-five, I met the man I would marry and have our children with.

Marriage—*been there, done that.*

MILESTONE BADGE EARNED: MARRIAGE

MILESTONE 5

From a very early age, my oldest son, Aaron, invented new words and funny sayings. He *loved* to read. One of his favorite books was *Oh, the Thinks You Can Think* by Dr. Seuss. Toward the end of the book, there are these green blobby creatures at the bottom of the right-hand page. He promptly named them Snot, Bot, Booger, and Brät. We couldn't get past this page in the book *without* him pointing to each of the green blobs and reciting their new names. Reading Dr. Seuss books always provided extra entertainment, so many crazy characters to rename. It still cracks us all up to say, "Snot, Bot, Booger, Brät!"

The townhome association we lived at when Aaron was very little had a wonderful elongated circular backyard where the backs of the buildings faced each other and the sidewalk wound in the back. Sidewalks also circled each of the home groupings. When Aaron learned to ride a bike, he would circle our area, going around and around, shouting, "Itsy bitsy tiny bit, itsy bitsy tiny bit, itsy bitsy tiny bit!"

Sometimes, now, while riding those giant clover leaf circles on the highway in my car, I sing out, "Itsy bitsy tiny bit, itsy bitsy tiny bit, itsy bitsy tiny bit." Give it a try. I promise it will relieve your stress, and you'll be one of the few drivers on the highway with a huge cheeky grin on your face!

Before our second son arrived, my husband's parents watched Aaron for a weekend. When we went to pick him up, my mother-in-law said to me, "Aaron told me that you *make* him eat sauerkraut sandwiches." I was dumbstruck. "Sauerkraut sandwiches? I don't make sauerkraut sandwiches." I was so puzzled. Why would he say such a thing? Then it hit me—The week before, I had made Reuben sandwiches for dinner for the first time, and he only remembered the sauerkraut! He *hated* sauerkraut.

Five years after Aaron, our son Evan arrived. The two of them have always been close, but they loved playing practical jokes on each other. Aaron liked to hide in places where he knew his brother would pass by. When Evan approached, Aaron would jump out and scream at the top of his lungs, "THE MUFFIN MAN!"

Oh, do you know the muffin man? I do. I raised him, and he still laughs about this with his brother.

Kids and pets seem like a natural fit during childhood. Cats, dogs, a borrowed lizard, fish, and finally, hamsters. After the boys found, to everyone's horror, half of a hamster and the other one looking a bit plumper, we never again brought home hamsters.

We named our first cat Cairo. One day, Cairo scratched Evan's upper lip with quite a gash. He took the cat over to the laundry chute in the wall, opened it, and began trying to shove poor Cairo down the small dark metal tunnel. "What are you doing?" I asked. He said, "I want a new cat!" The harder he tried to put the cat down the chute, the more that cat scrambled to spread out its four legs around that small opening. Every angle that Evan tried, that cat danced around that hole. We were in tears. He never did get that cat down the clothes chute.

Evan had a fish he named Big Blue when he was about five or six years old. In-between the two twin beds in his bedroom was a short dresser with a fish tank on top. This was Big Blue's home. It was a pretty nice set up for one fish. Greenery, cool rocks, and a treasure chest that opened and closed as it released bubbles from the bubbler that kept the water just right for Big Blue.

Our evening routine included the four B's. Bath, bedroom, book, and bedtime. One night, after the bath, we headed up to his bedroom to read a book. Evan would usually check out Big Blue before we began reading. However, on this night, his fish…was belly up.

Evan was in tears—his beloved Big Blue was no more.

It is one of those moments, as a parent, where you struggle on how to console, and how to handle your child's first experience with death. I comforted him, and then we talked about what he would want to do with Big Blue. Did he want to wait until tomorrow to bury him? Did he want to freeze him and think about it? Or did he want to go to the bathroom, say a few parting words for Big Blue, and have a burial at sea?

He chose burial at sea in the bathroom.

So, I turned off the bubbler in the fish tank and gently removed Big Blue with the net. We went into the bathroom, said a few words about what a great fish Big Blue had been, said a prayer, and flushed.

Whew! He appeared to be handling it just fine. We read our book, I tucked him in, and he drifted off to sleep.

The next night, we began our four B's routine. When we got to his bedroom upstairs, I realized that the fish tank was still there. We lay together on his bed and read our book. When the story was done, and with the bubbler shut off, the silence was a big reminder to Evan that Big Blue was gone…and he began to cry.

I tried to offer words of comfort to no avail. Evan said, "You don't understand. You have *never* lost someone you loved before!"

I explained to Evan that I had lost people I loved, and more recently, before he was born, my grandpa, his grandma's dad. I did my best to explain how that loss felt—and that I understood that his heart hurt. I also talked about being happy that one day I would see them in heaven.

Evan said, "So, your grandpa's in heaven?"

"Yes," I said.

With that, Evan abruptly sat up in bed, and with exaggerated hand gestures, he threw his hands upward, motioning toward the ceiling, and said loudly, "YOUR GRANDPA MAY BE IN HEAVEN." Then he brought his hands down, and beating his palms to his chest said, "BUT MY FISH…IS STUCK IN THE SEWER!!!"

I felt an enormous outburst of laughter welling up inside that I just couldn't keep down. While suppressing leaks and squeaks of laughter, I quickly tucked him in, kissed him goodnight, and headed quickly down the stairs, shut the stairway door, and burst out laughing.

Numerous other fish joined our household after Big Blue, but we *never, ever,* flushed another one down the toilet!

Morgan, our sock-loving golden retriever, joined the family and essentially grew up with the boys. If you were missing a pair of socks, the chances were good that she had them in her mouth, full of drool. We taught her many tricks: bang-bang, hide, and the boys, being Packer football fans, taught her to bark to "GO PACK GO!" During football games, they would shout "GO PACK GO!" and Morgan would bark three times with them. A true football mascot.

During a camping/portaging trip to the BWCA (Boundary Waters Canoe Area) in Northern Minnesota, Morgan capsized our boat. The portage into the wilderness on this first day of our vacation was very windy with high waves. She'd been laying on the floor behind Aaron in the front of the boat. I was sitting in the back and watched as Morgan stood up, looked over the edge, and in what felt like slow motion, caused the entire vessel to roll, depositing the three of us into a forty-five-foot deep bay.

My son, Aaron, and I were fine—we had life jackets on, and most of our gear was tied in. But Morgan would not leave our side and began to panic in the water. We had to turn the boat upside down, drag her onto the top of the turned over canoe and then float the boat and dog to shore. After that, she became very afraid of the water and wouldn't go in and retrieve anything. So, the boys and my nephew decided they were going to teach her to love the water again. The three boys took turns throwing sticks into the water and *retrieving* them. Before we knew it, Morgan joined in the fun and was back in the water...

One day, I came home from work to two laughing boys. They were older by this time, high school and junior high. Standing in front of Morgan, they told me they had a surprise. When they stepped aside, I saw Miss Morgan with a large "M" shaved onto her forehead. "SURPRISE!" they said, bursting out laughing. Yes, a surprise, and Morgan? She panted happily with that doggy smile. It took a long time for that "M" to grow out.

Aside from making up silly words when he was young, Aaron was precocious and full of practical jokes. One evening, after coming home from work, the front doorbell rang. I opened the door, and two neighborhood girls stood there. One of the little girls, being very quiet and shy, asked, "Can we have some tacos?"

"Tacos?" I said. "We don't have any tacos." She looked at her sister and looked back at me, and then they both quickly darted out of the yard. Thinking it was the neighborhood kids joking around, I didn't give it a second thought.

About fifteen minutes later, the doorbell rang again. This time I opened the door to find a man and his little kids. "We are here for the free tacos," he said with a big smile on his face.

"Free tacos?" I questioned.

"Yes," he said, "the free tacos!"

"I'm sorry," I said very confused. "We don't have free tacos." Was the entire neighborhood in on this joke?

The man looked perplexed, and then pointed to the front of our yard and said, "But the sign... ?" As I looked in the direction he was pointing, I saw a hockey stick stuck into our front lawn with a large poster board taped at the top. I went outside and then when I walked around to the front of the makeshift sign, I recognized the artwork and handwriting immediately: "FREE TACOS!"—*Aaron!*

He thought it would be funny to enlist his brother to help. One more group stopped by before he took the sign down. All I need to say to Aaron now is "FREE TACOS?" and he cracks up laughing.

I wanted my sons to grow up to be adventurous eaters —to be open-minded to new experiences in life. So, I served eggplant, avocados, Brussels sprouts, spinach, and lentils, not only for their health but to enjoy a wide variety of foods. I also selfishly loved trying new recipes, and I wanted to share these new creations without becoming a short-order cook, making several different meals a night around what they didn't like.

So, in an attempt to get them to try a variety of foods, I made up the *Forty Times* food rule. I would tell them, "Did you know that sometimes you have to try something forty times before you like it?" They believed me, and for the most part, it worked.

Don't get me wrong, we still had to jump over many food hurdles. The boys loved noodles, or as they both called them, "noo-noo's," and we had those days, weeks, and months where it was the only food they wanted for nourishment.

Then comes those moments where you are witness to change. During one summer vacation, we stopped at the historic Naniboujou Lodge on Minnesota's North Shore for dinner. The boys loved the dining rooms colorfully painted ceiling, its massive stone fireplace *and* its name. They laughed as they repeatedly tried to say Naniboujou – and before long, it was renamed *nanna-nanna-boo-jou*, and we *still* call it that! For his meal, Evan ordered a California burger that came with lettuce, tomato, onion, and avocado on it. His order surprised me because I knew he didn't care for onions. Without challenging or questioning his order, I sat back and waited to see what would happen.

When the waiter brought out our food, Evan's burger came with the bun top and the veggie toppings set to the side to self-assemble. He looked at his plate and asked loudly "Hey! Where're the onions?" As the waiter went back to the kitchen to retrieve the missing vegetable, I leaned toward him and asked, "Evan, you *want* onions?" Nodding his head, and with a big proud grin on that adorable face, he said, "Uh huh. I think I've had them forty times!"

He's eaten onions ever since.

My sons are grown now, and we try to get together often for a family game night that includes either grilling or cooking something fun together. A few years ago, during one of these family game nights, the conversation turned to their love of a wide range of foods: various blue or pungent cheeses, a wide variety of mushrooms, all types of vegetables, and fresh ways of cooking and exploring new culinary delights. They agreed that someday, when they have kids, they'd share the forty times rule.

I had to interrupt their musings and confess. "Wait... you both know I made up that rule, right?" I had *assumed* by this time in their lives that they had figured out that no one else had this rule.

They looked at each other in raised eyebrow, wide-eyed disbelief. Then they looked back at me and burst into laughter. "WHAT?!" They had NO idea! We still laugh over this.

Oh, and Aaron? Now in his late twenties, he recently shared with me that he now likes sauerkraut—he thinks he's had it forty times!

Motherhood is never what you expect and everything you did expect all rolled together. Whether it's pulling up a rug to have deep conversations, or when you roll your eyes and sigh, "When will this phase end?" Invariably, they do end, and in rapid succession.

One day you find yourself an empty nester recollecting treasured events from the past. Memories of flushing fish, an "M" shaved dog, "Free Tacos," half of a hamster, sauerkraut sandwiches, made up silly words, and cats in the laundry chute bubble to the surface and knowing you would do it all over again—forty times.

MILESTONE BADGE EARNED: MOTHERHOOD

MILESTONE 6

I've come full circle and would have never expected to be dating again in my fifties. A few friends said that they were living vicariously through me on this journey, that it appeared to be FUN! Yes *and* No. Unfortunately, dating in my fifties is a whole different ball game than when I was young. But with the coaxing of friends, I trekked into the whacky landscape of Internet dating.

Internet dating—what a *weird* concept. You scroll through screen after screen of strangers, viewing their profile photos and reading a wide range of originality in narratives. When you find someone who seems interesting, and the reaction is mutual, you begin chatting through secured communication. Then, if the interaction is going well, the next step is a phone call, with the possibility of meeting face-to-face.

Now I've made more than my fair share of blunders in entering this new dating scene. The first two or three dates I went on, I was at a loss for word. Absolutely paralyzed. In the *good old days*, you met someone, talked, made a connection, and *then* you dated. In this new technology-driven world of finding companionship, it's a succession of blind dates. I was either dressed too casual or too formal. I'd get very nervous—trying to remember how this dating dance works. By the fourth man I met, wine sounded like a good way to relax, but three glasses *don't* a good date make. Poor guy!

Eventually, what is new develops into something more comfortable. You connect more, set up dates, and start to enjoy the process, or, at least find the humor that leaves you saying: "You just can't make this stuff up!"

There came a time when I connected with someone, where it seemed our interests aligned, and we were mutually interested in each other. We shared our suspicions of online dating, wondering how honest people were in their profiles, and I expressed to him that I couldn't trust dating someone who posted misleading information. After all, it seemed ludicrous that anyone would misrepresent their profile—after all, if you were to eventually meet, they would obviously find out! Right? *Right…*

After spending a few weeks chatting back and forth, we finally set up a day to meet for dinner. He made reservations, and we agreed to meet at the bar of the restaurant. This would give us extra time to talk before being seated for dinner. Upon entering the eatery, I told the host that I was meeting someone and he shared that my date had told him to watch for a tall woman with very curly hair. *(Go figure!)* He pointed in the direction of the bar to where my date was waiting. At that moment, a man, *who I didn't recognize*, stood up and waved. I looked over my shoulder to see who this person was waving at, but there was no one standing behind me. *Perhaps he's trying to get the attention of some friends,* I thought.

As I drew nearer to the counter, trying to spot my date, the same man waved again. And again, I looked over my shoulder to see who he was signaling. As I turned my head back around, I wondered, *Hmmm, could this be…him?* By this time, he walked toward me and reached out to shake my hand. "Joni, it's so nice to meet you in person." I took a closer look. It *was* my date, but about twenty years older than his profile picture and about six inches shorter than his description.

It was a short date.

I then connected with a guy who appeared to share my love of the outdoors. He worked as an executive at a local corporation where an acquaintance of mine worked. I called her and asked if she knew anything about him. While she didn't know him, she knew of him and thought he was a nice guy, so I agreed to a date.

He wanted to take me horseback riding at the farm where he stabled some horses. I felt comfortable setting up a longer date because, after all, someone I knew, knew of him. It sounded like a wonderful afternoon.

As I kept watch out my living room window for my date to arrive, a car pulled up that I thought must belong to a teenager in the neighborhood. This red car was completely decked out with chrome wheels, a wide white stripe down the entire center of the car—trunk to hood—very flashy.

Out stepped a fifty-something man from that car. It was my date—and I *did* recognize him. When he got to my front door, the top of his shirt was unbuttoned, and he was sporting a gold chain around his neck. Wait! Did I just transport back to the 1970s? He *looked* like his profile picture, but the outdoor part of him was not jumping out at me.

On the ride to the farm, he talked nonstop about his career, *his money*, his toys, *his money*, his cars, *his money*, his horses, *his money*…you get the picture.

When we arrived at the farm, the owners came out to greet him. They said, "Hey, you look great. You've lost a lot of weight!" He put his arm around my shoulder, squeezed, and said, "That's what the love of a good woman can do for you."

Keep in mind, this was our *first* date.

A few minutes later, the wife reminded him that she needed the last few months of boarding rent…*Hmmm.*

The horseback ride was a lot of fun, but the conversation revolved around…you guessed it…money and toys and more money and more toys, and then a little about his kids and his divorce, and I was relieved when we started back.

Suddenly, he grabbed the reins of my horse to lead us into the barn, pulling my horse behind his. This would have been fine, and I'm sure he did it to be kind, but the speed we were going left me with no time to *duck* my head before entering the side barn door.

Now I had a goose egg in the middle of my forehead.

After we changed clothes and before heading out for a light meal we had planned, he said, "I want to take you to this really nice steak place. It's called Pittsburgh Blue, and they have the best steaks you will ever taste." I told him that I just wanted a light salad, someplace casual, and then head home. But, he was persistent. "Come on! It'll be great, the steaks just melt in your mouth, and the other food they have is excellent. I really want to take you there."

I agreed—I had nothing to lose, and a good steak and a glass of wine would taste pretty good about now.

The restaurant was nice—and pricey. He ordered an *expensive* bottle of red wine and a jumbo shrimp cocktail appetizer. For dinner, I chose their filet and asparagus. He ordered the bone-in filet, three sides—*another* shrimp appetizer and a second bottle of wine. The dinner conversation was much better, and as he started polishing off the second shrimp appetizer, I had a chance to share a little about my sons and my life.

And he was right, the steak was absolutely *amazing*.

I couldn't finish everything on my plate, so he reached over, helped himself, and finished my meal. No doggy bag for Joni.

When the waitress handed him the bill, he opened it, and just kept staring at it. He looked up at me, then down at the bill, then glanced back up at me, and then down at the bill again.

Now, keep in mind, *I* wanted to go someplace for a light meal. This was *his* invitation, *his idea*.

The bill in hand, glancing back up at me, he was, for the first time—speechless—frozen.

And what I said next, I wish I could've taken back. "Are you looking for me to pay this?" And without skipping a beat, he set the bill on the table, turned it around, and pushed it toward me and said, "Could you?" Now I was speechless. *Really?!*

At this point, I just wanted to get home. I paid the bill, *a small fortune*, and he drove me home.

In my driveway, he started talking about setting up another date. I turned toward him, extended my right arm, and pointing my index finger down, made a circling motion between us and said, "This…." Then I raised my index finger upward, and moving it from side to side, said, "Will never happen again!" I left the car and went into my home. I peeked out the living room window, and my date was still sitting there, and he remained there for quite some time—I'm sure, not having any clue as to why there would be no future date.

I kept the restaurant receipt, showing it to friends and coworkers that Monday. After a few years, I finally lost track of it. And yes, that *never* happened again!

MILESTONE BADGE EARNED: DATING—*AGAIN*

MILESTONE 7

ENTERING THE WHITE CHAIR DAYS ~ WHERE IT ALL BEGAN.

    Wait, White Chair Days? Back up, *what* is a White Chair Day? Ah, herein lies the story. I woke up one morning with a déjà vu feeling that some sort of weird puberty had hit me, once again. "What is this? What is going on?"
    I had this very strong sensation that I had experienced this very awkward feeling before. Except, this time around, I *wish* I was back down to a size AA bra, and when I stare in the mirror, I laugh out loud at the thought of my

Hershey candy bar diet of my youth. I think I found those candy bars on my thighs! I have also grown accustomed to not only my freckles, but my curls, and I quit trying to tame them years ago. Like parts of my body, they fall where they will.

While puberty has a period of stumbling over your feet and through life, this time around, my brain, body, and mouth were completely out of sync. They had a mind of their own.

Not only that, but I was *doing* crazy things. Like in at beginning of this story, me not remembering what I walked into the room to get…"Oh, yes, that's right, KEYS." I have heard the stories of keys in the fridge, etc., but I just didn't think it would ever happen to me…until I found a very cold set of car keys next to the skim milk I picked up the night before from the store. "UGH!"

I can retain water with ease, but retaining my thoughts?

About a month before a big milestone birthday, words would fly out of my mouth opposite of what I wanted to say. Up was down, right was left, green was blue, and when I wanted to use the correct word to express what I was stumbling to say, the word was gone. VANISHED! "You know, that thing-a-ma-jig, that whatcha-ma-call-it, that thingy…" My thoughts felt like a screen saver had just turned on in my brain—a blank screen came up, and someone had pressed "delete" on those thought pop-ups.

I felt embarrassed, and although I nervously laughed and joked about it, at the time, I felt like this was only happening to me. And remember the forty times rule I made up with my sons? Now they were telling me that they had to tell me something forty times before I would remember it!

About a week before this milestone birthday, I drove coworkers out for lunch to a local restaurant. On the way back to the office, I approached a right hand turning lane that I needed to merge into. In the middle of the turning lane, I noticed a green, plastic garbage can lid that must have blown off a nearby trash can.

I said, *out loud*, "Oh, no! There's a white chair in the road!"

Yes…I said *white chair*…

My coworkers burst into laughter. "Joni, WHERE did you get white chair from?" They continued to laugh not only all the way back to the office but for days to come.

For the life of me, and to this day, I have absolutely *no idea* where the words *white chair* came from. I *know* I saw a green garbage can lid on the road, but why did I *say*, "White chair?"

When that milestone birthday arrived, we headed outside to go to lunch to celebrate. Taped to the back of my car trunk was a sign that a coworker had drawn on large printing paper. He'd drawn and colored a green garbage can lid and a white chair. On the top of this large sign were the words: I'm a green garbage can lid, NOT a white chair!

And sitting behind my parked car sat a small, white Adirondack chair. Got to love those coworkers.

I began to share my "White Chair Day" story with friends, family, colleagues, business contacts, and acquaintances. And as I shared my story, others started to share their White Chair Day stories with me.

I enjoyed getting a call from someone who would say, "Joni, I just had a White Chair Day," and then proceed to share their story. There was comfort in hearing these stories. Not only would they help me understand that I'm not alone during these White Chair Days, but in some very good company.

Milestone badge earned? The biggest milestone of all, finding the humor in all of it.

MILESTONE BADGE EARNED: MY WHITE CHAIR DAYS

Enjoy these White Chair Day stories.

#1 - WRONG RAILING

Jackie owned a brokerage agency, and my company worked with her not only as our agent of record but also as our benefits administrative representative. I looked forward to our meetings because Jackie always brought entertaining updates on her life—her husband, family, grandchildren, and the numerous house moves they made. Stories of her humorous escapades lightened the otherwise serious business discussions.

Work and leisure time took Jackie to many places. One day she traveled to Kalispell in northwest Montana for a client presentation. Kalispell has incomparable beauty and sits in the Flathead Valley in the heart of the Rocky

Mountains. Arriving flights into Glacier Park International Airport unload passengers directly onto the tarmac where they are met with one of the most beautiful landing strip views in the country. Passengers are then taken by a shuttle to the small terminal.

Boarding the vehicle, Jackie took a seat near the rear exit door and immediately engaged in lively conversation with fellow travelers seated to her right as the remaining passengers made their way on board.

Full of life, Jackie's conversations are always an enjoyable experience. She's animated and does as much speaking with her hands as she does with her mouth. Hand gestures punctuate expressions, and the inflections in her voice bring a story to life.

As the shuttle started to move, Jackie continued her conversation—her right-hand gesturing along with the conversation while she instinctively grabbed the railing to the left of her seat.

As the shuttle lumbered toward the terminal, she felt the railing shift. She gripped a little tighter while continuing her lively conversation. When it moved again, she clutched even tighter. All of a sudden, she felt the rail swing away, jerking her abruptly to the left. She looked over to see what was going on.

To her horror, the railing she'd been clinging to was not a handrail at all but the leg of a very slender man standing beside her!

#2 – HOW DRY I AM

A chilly summer day; overcast skies and heavy dark clouds threaten to unleash a drenching rainstorm. This type of weather doesn't bode well for a short five-mile jaunt to the grocery store, but Joy needed to pick up a few things. After all, it was only rain—what could go wrong?

Keeping her eyes on the sky, Joy drove down the street to her local grocery. Even though it was still dry when she arrived at the store, the thickness of the air suggested that it wouldn't remain that way for much longer. Once inside the market, she quickly hunted out the items on her list. Groceries were paid for, packed up, and loaded into the van, and still no rain—whew!

As she took a moment to catch her breath before the trip home, the thunder rumbled, and the skies opened. Lightning flashed. Giant raindrops rang out like the beat of a percussion drum, getting louder and faster with every blow on the metal roof.

It was pouring outside.

As Joy leaned back in the driver's seat, eyes closed, listening to the soothing rhythm of the rain, a thought suddenly struck her. "I don't have an umbrella or a raincoat with me! I've got to get home!"

She pulled into her driveway in front of their two-stall, detached garage. She sat there wondering, "How on earth am I going to make it into the house without getting drenched?" She remembered that she had a blue raincoat hanging next to the back door inside the garage, but that didn't help her sitting in the driveway.

With her husband Mark home, she called him from her cell phone for help. "Honey, do you think you could bring me the raincoat from the garage? It is pouring outside, and I don't want to get soaked."

He started laughing. "Yeah, right! I'm supposed to run to the garage in this downpour to get you a raincoat while you stay nice and dry in the van?"

Joy's response was, "Well, yeah!"

Her husband laughed so hard he could hardly get his next words out.

"Joy, how about you do this. Use the garage door opener, open the garage door, and drive your van into that nice dry garage. Then put on that blue raincoat hanging by the back door, and you will stay dry as you walk to the house!"

#3 – KEPT IN THE DARK

Our lives have turned into busy snares. Lunch breaks are sprint sessions of squeezing in a list of never-ending errands: groceries, pet food, a gift for an upcoming birthday, an oil change, library returns, picking up a prescription, getting cash, tires rotated, and as soon as one item is crossed off, another takes its place. It's no wonder that in this whirlwind of fast living, we can literally drive into a White Chair Day.

On a busy noon break, after realizing she hadn't packed a lunch, Joni decided to go to a local drive-thru and order a salad. It would be something quick and healthy to bring back to the office and quickly wolf down while eating over a keyboard or juggling the phone receiver.

The drive-thru line was long and moving as fast as a snail on a salt lick. As Joni waited, she tried to remember what type of salads the restaurant offered on its menu, and as usual, her mind began to wander.

When did drive-thrus first start? She remembered the A&W drive-in, with tall frosted glasses of foamy root beer floats. She then remembered she needed to pick up a wedding gift, and didn't she have a marketing presentation due? Oh, and she needed to call a plumber about the slow kitchen sink leak, and…

She heard a horn honk, signaling that daydream time was over, and she inched her car forward to order. As she pulled up, she noticed that the board was dark—no lights at all. "They must be having trouble with their sign. Maybe that's why the line has taken so long."

Just then a very young, sweet sounding gal's voice came over the speaker: "Welcome to Wendy's, may I take your order?"

"Yes," Joni said. "I know that I want to order a salad, but I can't remember what kind of salads you have. Could you please turn on your menu so I can see the choices? The sign is black."

There was a slight pause, and then Joni heard laughter emanating from the speaker. The sweet young gal, trying to compose herself, asked, "Ma'am, are you wearing polarized sunglasses?"

"Well, yes," said Joni, "but what does that have to do with salads?" She was perplexed. *What an odd question to ask.*

Then, the young woman said, "Ma'am, please take off your sunglasses…"

At this point, Joni was confused but complied with the request. Sliding her polarized sunglasses down her nose, the menu magically appeared!

OMG! I'm Having a White Chair Day | 47

#4 – JUST A LITTLE TO THE LEFT

There was an iced tea company who modified the design of their glass bottles to give their customers a better grip. The right side of the container had four indentations for fingers, and the left side contained an indentation for your thumb. The instructions recommended shaking the iced tea well before drinking in order to combine all of the flavors.

Lila grabbed one of the iced teas during a break at work. The added indentations helped prevent the wet, perspiring bottle from catapulting out of her hands like a liquid filled missile. "It is so smart that someone thought enough to embed these impressions into the glass bottle," she said as she vigorously shook the tea.

Now, Lila is a person with a huge heart. As she stood shaking her drink with her right hand, a thought occurred and her internal reflections became verbal. "I feel really awful for people who are left-handed. What do they do when they need to shake this iced tea?"

Without skipping a beat, a coworker slipped the bottle out of her right hand, and turning the bottle around ninety degrees, placed it into her left hand, where all the indents lined up perfectly.

#5 - SOUL FOOD

Wearing shoes versus a good pair of sturdy winter boots on ice-covered streets makes for some risky, yet comical performances—along with a few broken bones. That's why Joni wears boots to work and brings a change of shoes in a separate bag.

Lesson learned: Ice and Joni don't mix.

One crisp morning after arriving at work, Joni realized that she'd left her shoe bag at home. "Darn! Now, I'll have to wear my clunky snow boots all day."

She'd a mid-morning meeting their bankers for a review of the company 401k plan. Now while these mid-year reviews are necessary, they can also leave your eyes glazed over and your head spinning from lengthy discussions about expense ratios, market conditions, diversified investment portfolios, and fiduciary responsibilities. Walking into the conference with snow boots might just add the right amount of comic relief.

"Are you cold?" the account rep asked, glancing at her boots.

"Nope. I just thought the conversation might get a bit deep," she replied.

The meeting ended just before lunch, and Joni headed to the break room. The room is a busy place during lunch with a continual buzz of people weaving in and out and around each other getting dishes, utensils, and jockeying for position in the microwave line. Adding a pair of clunky winter boots to this kitchen dance makes for very awkward maneuvers. After grabbing her thermal lunch bag from her office, Joni waited for her turn to warm up her leftovers.

As her turn for the microwave neared, she opened her bag and found—her shoes! Cold, sole food for lunch!

That evening, Joni found her lunch exactly where she'd left it that morning…on the rug by the back-patio door—where her shoes normally sit.

#6 – THE DANCING SPRAYER

Dodie's car really needed a wash down. Covered with dirty spring slush, her vehicle looked more like a metallic pig and a technological conveyance. While there are newer, more modern touchless automatic car washes, Dodie chose the semi-high-tech, do-it-yourself coin-operated option. You know the kind; you drive into individual concrete-covered tunnels, park, get out, deposit the correct number of coins needed for the wash cycle selected, grab the trigger gun, and start washing and waxing your car.

The building was filled with busy motorists washing winter grime off their vehicles, so Dodie smiled as she slipped into one of the last remaining empty stalls. Once parked, she dug through her purse for change.

While some self-serve washers accept credit cards, this particular business didn't. Fortunately, Dodie knew that the manager's office contained a change machine, so she headed to the small building where she exchanged her dollar bills for a handful of coins.

Dodie mentally counted out the number of coins needed as she walked back to her stall: *fifty…seventy-five…a dollar…a dollar twenty-five…*

When she reached her stall, she grabbed the trigger gun, deposited her carefully counted coins in the payment box and flipped the switch. The nozzle immediately began to shoot out a powerful streaming mix of water and sudsy cleaning solution. She then turned around to start washing her car—but it was GONE!

In a panic, she dropped the spray nozzle to the floor. The force of the streaming water sent the wand bouncing across the empty concrete floor. Dodie didn't have a cell phone, so she raced back to the manager's office for help.

As she passed adjacent stalls, she cried out for help. "My car has been stolen! Help, my car has been stolen!" Of course, motorists wanted to help her, and she now had a small string of concerned individuals joining her on the way to the manager's office.

She provided the manager a detailed description of her car as they walked back to the empty stall. As they passed the very next stall, Dodie stopped dead in her tracks.

There was her car.

And in the adjacent bay—the dropped spray nozzle continued to dance across the floor.

#7 – NOW WHERE DID I PUT THAT?

No one can deny the incredible advancement technology makes each year. Computers, once requiring entire rooms, can now fit into the palm of your hand. The same applies to the lowly computer mouse. New computer models come with touchscreen ability, and while they are convenient, for the person lacking toothpick-thin fingers, accessing data can be somewhat of a frustrating challenge.

Fortunately, Joni's touchscreen computer came with a stylus pen. The pencil-like instrument that works like a finger yet is more accurate and never leaves smudges of food, lotion, and finger oil on your computer screen.

One evening, while working on a project, she received an incoming call from her friend, Dave. Wanting to concentrate on their conversation, Joni reached for the stylus to click to save her work and close the program, but it was gone.

"Dave, when my phone was ringing, I saved my work using the stylus. I know I did, but now I can't find it!" she said as she walked through the rooms, phone to ear, searching for the missing implement.

As they continued to talk, Joni grabbed a flashlight and looked on the chair, under the couch, under the foot stool, under the cushion, on the rug…everywhere. Finally, she came up for air and said, jokingly, "Dave, I think YOU took my stylus!"

After their call, Joni remembered her grown sons would be stopping by that night after seeing a movie. *I think I'll enlist their young eyes. After all, it couldn't have gone far—I'm sure they'll find it right away.*

After her sons had arrived, the boys thoroughly investigated their mother's work area, but the implement was nowhere to be found. Joni resigned herself that her stylus had met the same mysterious fate as that of missing socks.

After lunch the next day, she entered the kitchen to rinse her plate and put it in the dishwasher. As she bent down to place her fork in the utensil holder, she stopped. There, amongst the spoons and forks was a black stick—her stylus!

#8 – SO JUMPY

Long before cell phones, people relied on pagers, also referred to as "beepers," to keep in touch with work staff. The person carrying the pager had the choice of either an audible beep or pulsing vibration to inform them of an incoming message that displayed on a tiny screen with a phone number or small message, such as "Call Home."

Lynne worked for a company whose entire staff carried pagers. After one of their weekly sales meetings, some of the staff stayed behind to socialize.

At some point, the conversation shifted to a dialogue about people who are jumpy. It's not easy being a nervous person. Unexpected surprises can send them flying out of their seats, and, unfortunately, jumpy people are targets for those who enjoy seeing their startled reactions.

During the conversation, Lynne, knowing her co-worker's excitabilities, said, "Oh, you should see Kelly jump whenever her *vibrator* goes off."

"LYNNE!" a startled Kelly screamed as everyone roared with laughter.

For a long time, whenever Lynne's pager vibrated, she held an extra special smile on her face remembering jumpy Kelly.

#9 – WHERE IS SHE GOING?

The mayhem that transpires when a group of women get together! It's a time to throw diets out the window, laugh so hard that no noise comes out, but pee does, and discover that suffering from a lack of sleep makes everything funnier.

A group of sisters traveled one weekend to Duluth, MN, for a girls' getaway of leisure. It poured on the second night of their vacation, but the sisters were still eager to head out for an enjoyable dinner. One sister, Anne, said, "Let me use the bathroom first, and I'll meet you guys in the car."

The hotel had a couple of parking lots, and it was easy to get turned around. While the two sisters waited in the running car, they glimpsed through the heavy rain, the outline of their sister running toward them.

Anne concentrated on moving quickly to keep from getting soaked, and when she reached the car, she yanked open the back door and jumped in.

As she shook off the excess water and moved her hair out of her eyes, she glanced up. Staring back at her was a large dog and two men she didn't know.

The men looked at each other, the confused dog cocked his head, and Anne's eyes became the size of saucers. "Oh, this isn't my car!" And with that, she got out as quickly as she got in.

When she finally made it to the right car, her sisters were howling with laughter. "We weren't sure *who* you were leaving with!"

"You could've yelled out the window and stopped me!" Anne said.

"What would be the fun in that?"

#10 - MAN-TEE-HOSE!

Years ago, there was a nylon generation. In most office situations, women had to wear either a dress or a skirt with a suit jacket to work. This meant wearing nylons or pantyhose was a *required* necessary evil.

Nylons weren't cheap, so women needed to find inventive ways to stretch their stocking budget. Prone to tearing one could easily ruin a perfectly good pair of pantyhose in seconds, leaving your leggings with one good leg and one bad leg.

Hester wisely came up with a creative solution to this conundrum. If her nylons had a run in one leg, she'd simply cut off the bad leg and be left with a brief and one good stocking. She'd then repeat this process every time only one leg was ruined.

Making lemonade out of lemons, Hester would wear two pairs of one-legged hose. Two one-legs equaled one perfectly good pair of nylons. Brilliant!

One morning, Hester had a sales training meeting of which she was one of the presenters to a mostly male audience. She stood at the front of the room, sailing through her presentation. Success!

When done with the meeting, she exited the conference room and suddenly felt a strange sensation against her calves. She looked down, and to her horror, saw a third leg dangling between her legs!

Mortified, she ran into the nearest office, shut the door, and shouted to the man behind the desk, "Quick, I need some scissors!" Grabbing the shears from the surprised manager, she hiked up her skirt just enough to expose her third leg and cut it off.

From that day forward, Hester's third leg episode became wittily referred to as her "man-tee-hose" day!

#11 – HAIR RAISING EXPERIENCE

Years ago, some companies required all female sales professionals with long tresses to wear their hair up, whether by tying their hair back in a polished ponytail or putting it up in a ballerina bun, French twist, knot, or some other raised style.

In a hurry, Hester applied her physical flexibility to avoid ruining her hair in the morning's heavy mist. While most people can't reach down and touch their toes, Hester's movements resembled that of a skilled contortionist, her body bending in all directions as she popped in and out of her open car doors, grabbing stuff.

Completing a couple more acrobatic moves, Hester placed her planner into her briefcase and then set it along with her purse on the ground just before shutting the car door.

Thud! As soon as the car door shut, Hester's head jerked backward—a portion of her hair now caught in the closed door!

Hester didn't know how she'd managed to get into such a predicament, but there she was, bent backward, hair caught in a locked car door. Her thoughts raced. *Oh, my gosh. Does anyone see me? How am I going to get out of this?* Although awkward and uncomfortable, she tried to crouch lower to remain out of sight.

Out of the corner of her eye, Hester saw her purse, right where she'd placed it on the ground, not more than a foot from her. "If I can just get my keys, I can open the door and be free." Twisting, she reached down, stretching as far as she could without pulling out her hair by the root, but her bag remained out of reach. Trying another tactic, she tried to snag the bag with her foot, but there was no way to lift the small purse handles up enough to grab them.

Gently twisting, trying to free her captured hair, the contortionist now attempted to turn into an escape artist, but Houdini she was not! *What am I going to do?*

Hester started to feel like a soggy, human pretzel. "Well, I can't stay here." She took several deep breaths. Holding her hair in her left hand to prevent scalping, she turned and tugged once more to try to free her locks. No luck. Frustrated, Hester twisted toward her torturer and reached for the door handle to confirm what she already knew—the door was locked.

As she reached out, she heard the unmistakable jingle and stared in disbelief. There, in her right hand were her car keys.

#12 - ALARMING

Lynne works for a company that spends an enormous amount of time attending face-to-face meetings. There's nothing more effective when you're trying to land a new customer. Getting to the point where a prospect accepts an in-person meeting is challenging to secure, but once scheduled, it's a time to make a good first impression.

Lynne was out on one of these sales calls with a team member. Arriving early, they parked in front of the business where the meeting was scheduled—close to the main entrance and several large windows.

Sitting in the car, they took the extra time to prepare. There is more to these meetings than looking the part and being polished and professional. Before going in, they reviewed the account needs and struggles, and then shut off electronic devices to eliminate any possible noise distractions. After all, the customer is the first priority.

Feeling very prepared and confident, they got out of the car.

As soon as they shut the car doors, the car's security alarm shrieked its fast, high-pitch squeal. "WEEoooWEEoooWEEooo!"

Quickly scrambling back into the car, they shut the doors and frantically tried to shut off the alarm. Eventually disabling it, the blare of the alarm was replaced with the noise of giggling.

Talk about making an entrance! They waited a few minutes before venturing out. Once again, as soon as they shut the car doors, the alarm went off. They scrambled back into the car, and of course, by this time, were laughing hysterically!

Looking up, they could see they were attracting an audience. Staff from the prospective customer started gathering at the windows to see what was going on. Wiping away tears and trying to compose themselves, they realized that enough time had passed, and they really needed to go in for the meeting.

They opened the doors, and sure enough, the alarm went off again! This time they remained inside the car. In some unknown combination of turning on and off the vehicle, hitting the lock and unlock button several times, Lynne's team member was finally able to disable the alarm once and for all.

This unusual entrance appeared to have had an impact. When introduced to the person they were meeting with, Lynne's team member handed him her business card. As they talked and laughed about their grand entrance, he unconsciously rolled her business card up in his hand.

He then asked, "Do you have a business card I could get from you?" Laughing, she nodded toward his hand.

#13 – HOW LOW CAN YOU GO?

> *Pantyhose come in an overabundance of options: control top, nude toe, reinforced toe, super shaper, no seam, and so on. Pantyhose, as the name implies, are hose with a waist-high brief that the package advertises as a "comfortable reinforced panty," but it is anything but comfy.*

One day while out shopping, Lynne found a pair of stockings that were thigh high. *Oh, what a great idea*, she thought. *If I buy these, I won't have to be bound in full pantyhose all day!*

This new find was a wonderful alternative to the traditional pantyhose. She could just simply pull these up beyond her skirt line and forget about them. No more uncomfortable brief digging into her waistline. "Why didn't I see these before?" she wondered. And with that, she eagerly purchased this new novelty.

The next morning, like a kid putting on a new back-to-school outfit, Lynne happily slipped on her new stockings.

Upon arriving at work, she started to descend the stairs to her office. One of the gentlemen she worked with joined her and struck up a conversation. As they continued down the stairs, Lynne felt an odd, tickling sensation on her right leg—her stocking was starting to slip down!

She resisted the urge to reach down and pull it back up. Instead, she quickened her pace, hoping she could make it to her office before her male coworker discovered her embarrassment. As the stocking continued to slip, she got a heightened sense of her surroundings, and Lynne realized a group of men were walking behind them.

At the bottom of the stairs, they continued down the hallway. The farther they walked, the more the stocking slipped, until it was a puddle around her ankle, in clear view of the male spectators behind her.

Lynne's face turned beet red. The coworker, oblivious to her plight, continued to talk with her. As soon as she could, she made a quick exit to the bathroom to pull up the stocking, followed by another quick exit to leave work to buy the *traditional* pantyhose. *What went wrong? Why didn't these new hose work?*

Driving to the store, it occurred to her. "Garter belt, I needed a garter belt!"

#14 – WHICH VAN IS IT ANYWAY?

One beautiful summer afternoon, Joy and two co-worker friends decided to go out to lunch. They had a favorite local restaurant that had a great salad bar, and the typical lunch question amongst the three was, "Do you feel like a salad today?"

Yes, this was a salad day!

It also happened to be one of those days where every conversation struck a funny bone with the group. As Joy drove, the contagious laughter in her van followed them into the restaurant.

Between trips to the salad bar, they chatted and laughed about marriage, dating at an older age, the escapades of their kids, and the humor of life in general. After paying their tabs, the women happily walked out into the parking lot to Joy's vehicle, continuing to laugh and chat along the way.

Joy climbed into the driver's seat of her blue van as one friend sat down in the passenger seat, and the other, opening the side sliding door, sat down. A quiet rushed over them as something just felt *strange*.

The first friend, noticing a lamp on the passenger's side floor, asked, "I don't remember this lamp, Joy. Where did you buy this?" Shortly after that, the second friend asked, "Um, Joy? Why do you have a baby seat back here?" Joy's sons were teenagers.

They just sat there…dumbstruck. Suddenly, one of the friends asked, "Is this your van?" It took several more seconds of staring at each other and looking around the interior before they simultaneously leapt from the vehicle.

Between shrieks of laughter and them voicing, "Oh, my gosh!" along with "Holy crap," the trio crept away from the identical blue, out-of-state licensed van, ducking low to avoid detection as they ran to Joy's van.

As they drove out of the parking lot, red-faced embarrassment gave way to hysterical laughter. Continually looking over their shoulders should their mistaken car escapade be discovered, Joy said, "This is by far one of my favorite lunch memories."

#15 – SOGGY BABY DOLL

According to an article in the New York Times (2016) entitled "The End of the Office Dress Code," corporate identity has given way to personal expression. Between employees tethered to work 24/7 by technology, and the expectation of always being available, work and home dress have blended. In an effort to have employees more comfortable, the once casual Friday eventually gave way to casual every day.

    Dressing in a way that makes her feel beautiful boosts Joy's mood and leaves her feeling positive and confident. Usually days before her monthly cycle starts, she feels a bit weepy. A song on the radio produces tears, an in-depth conversation with a friend leaves her tearful, and her high school son scoring a goal at his hockey game can bring her heart right into her throat in milliseconds.

On a particular Friday, Joy was in one of those sensitive moods and decided to dress up to combat the emotions. She put on a pretty, short sleeve, lace baby-doll top with satin ties in the back. Since it was a cold January morning, she added a dressy black jacket for added warmth.

Joy eased into her day, and by mid-morning had found her stride, becoming very productive. Around four o'clock in the afternoon, she took a break and headed to the restroom.

There was a female coworker in the bathroom stall next to her, and she commented that she thought Joy's boots were cute. They joked back and forth between the divide as they took care of business.

When Joy stood up from the toilet, she noticed a stream of water dripping off the left side of the seat and onto the floor. She hadn't felt wet on her left leg, dress pants, or undergarment. She turned around, searching for the answer as to where the water was coming from. Flabbergasted, she glanced up to see if anything was dripping from the ceiling.

Joy exited the stall and shared her confused, watery experience with a coworker who was washing her hands. Inexplicably, Joy reached behind her to feel the back of her jacket. Her hands moved downward, and suddenly she felt two wet dangling satin ties.

"YUCK!" she shouted. Her face flushed with embarrassment as she realized part of her wardrobe was now urine soaked. She burst into nervous laughter.

Trying to make Joy feel better, her coworker said, "At least it was your *own* pee and not someone else's!"

Joy stripped the shirt off, washed the ties in the bathroom sink and spent the rest of the afternoon at her desk, out of sight, and away from questions as to why her baby doll ties were wet.

#16 – LET'S PUT A LITTLE LIGHT ON THE SUBJECT

Cars are becoming one of the most complex gadgets that we own. Touchscreens, Bluetooth, navigation systems, self-parking, and the technology keeps expanding. All vehicles come with an owner's manual, but much like the instructions for other electronic devices, who reads them? Especially when it comes to cars—who reads the manual?

One night, after having dinner with a friend, Joni got into her car to drive home. As she left the parking lot, she noticed that the entire dashboard was dark—no lights at all.

She pulled the car to the side of the road. Her car has a push-button keyless start; no key is required to start up the car. So, thinking her car could be much like a home computer where you are told to *restart* the computer.

She pushed the button to shut off the car, waited a few minutes, and then turned it back on to see if the dashboard lights would now work. No luck. "Dang computer gremlins!" She tried shutting the car off and on again a few more times with the same result—a dark dashboard.

She needed to drive home, but how was she going to see the dashboard? She could do without seeing the radio, but she wouldn't be able to gauge the speed she was driving. She reached above her head and pressed the button to turn on the cabin lights. Though not the safest or best way to drive home, it helped her to see the speedometer, and it was her only option.

The next morning, she called the dealership to make an appointment to get her car in for repair. They couldn't get her car in for three more days. It was a long time to wait without dashboard lights.

However, Joni thought about it. "It is summer, and it is light outside when I drive to work, and still light out when I drive home." So, she thought she would be okay until the repair.

The night before the service appointment, Joni needed to run to the store, but what to do about the dark dashboard? Joni loves hiking and camping and has been called the camping "gadget queen." She has one of those headlamps that has an adjustable headband with a light that faces forward on your forehead.

She thought, *I'll just wear that! It is dark outside, and when I glance down at the dashboard, the small light will point down, and I'll be able to see my speed.* She hoped that no one she knew saw her driving like this, but it was dark, and it was better than having the cab lights on.

The next morning, she brought the car to the dealership. She explained to the technician how one night the dashboard just stopped working. He climbed into the driver's seat and pushed the button to start the car. He examined the dark dashboard and asked if she'd noticed trouble with any of the other lights in the car.

"No, nothing," she said. He then reached his hand toward the console, and gripping the trip meter lever on the dashboard, the one that resets trip mileage and many other dashboard items, turned it to the right.

And as he did…the dashboard lights magically turned back on and became brighter the more he turned the lever.

The first thing that crossed Joni's mind? That owner's manual!

#17 – A PEACEFUL STORM

In the transition from winter to spring the melting snow coincides with rain, and as the dirt washes away and puddles form, the first flowers reveal themselves. It is fun to remain young at heart and jump and splash in an occasional puddle, but on the roads, they coat our cars with waves of water and spring dirt from passing motorists.

On a warmer, drier spring day, Joni decided to take her vehicle to the car wash.

She *LOVES* the car wash. It has the same soothing effect on her as a rolling thunderstorm—and she *LOVES* thunderstorms!

Rainstorms start with that refreshing scent of precipitation—the air just smells fresh and clean. You can hear the light rumble of thunder in the distance, and then the rhythm of the rain slowly picks up in intensity. As the droplets become larger and increase in momentum, the splash hitting the windows is soothing, helping her to unwind. The winds sing, and the storm impacts Joni's mood, rinsing everything clean, including washing away any stress.

A car wash has that same hypnotic effect. It starts with the refreshing fragrance of a light spray starting at the front of the car, then you hear the rumble of the buffing cloths beginning to move in the distance, and the spray picks up in intensity. As the droplets hit the roof of the car, its soothing rhythm does its magic.

Joni looked forward to trips to the car wash and enjoyed what she referred to as her own personal mini rain storm.

It was a sunny day, and as she waited in line, she closed her eyes to soak in its warmth. The line was taking longer than usual, indicating that many of the drivers must have selected the deluxe car wash package.

In-between moving up in line, she continued to soak up the warm sunshine. Finally, her turn arrived, and of course, she selected the *longest* wash possible—the deluxe! She drove forward until the sign lit up red and displayed *STOP.* As soon as she stopped, the back-garage door rolled down, and the wash automatically began.

As the first drops of spray hit the front of her car, she closed her eyes to inhale that fresh, clean scent and listen to the rumble of the buffing clothes beginning to roar. The tap, tap, taps of the spray hitting the window grew with intensity, lifting her away to a place she can only call bliss.

Then, her peaceful rainstorm took on knocking thuds.

She opened her eyes to see a man standing outside the driver's window, trying to wake her up. Joni had fallen asleep in the car wash!

#18 – BALLS, BALLS, AND MORE BALLS

Getting together to celebrate birthdays and life events is common amongst girlfriends. One group of girlfriends would try to pick new places to eat and try new things when celebrating each of their birthdays.

For Lila's birthday, she chose to go bowling at a local bowling alley. This bowling alley has lots of lights, music, and video screens. A very fun and interactive place where the girlfriends could celebrate their friend's birthday while enjoying appetizers and a few drinks while bowling.

They paid for and were given their sexy bowling shoes—you know the ones—worn red, blue, and off-white or tan colors. Slippery to help you slide while bowling, but slippery enough to land you on your tailbone if you aren't careful!

This bowling alley color-coded all their bowling balls by weight. For example, the red balls were eight pounds, blue balls ten pounds, and so on. This color by weight system made it easy to locate the bowling ball you wanted.

The ladies settled in their lane, put on their shoes, and set out to find just the right bowling ball that would bring them that desired strike. Gina went to a section that was a bit farther away with more bowling balls to choose from.

Lynne was still trying to find a ball that felt like the right weight. She saw Gina and shouted out to her.

"Hey, Gina, what *color* are those *green* balls?"

And without missing a beat, Gina replied, "Twelve pounds!"

#19 – START YOUR ENGINES?

Suz's niece had been watching her younger children during the summer. It allowed the cousins time to connect, but it also solved the difficult task of trying to find a daycare since school had finished for the year.

As the summer wound down, Suz wanted to express her gratitude to her niece by taking her out for a nice dinner. Not only is it invigorating to treat yourself to a meal you don't have to prepare, but just getting out of the house to enjoy a refreshing and fun conversation makes a BIG difference.

Her husband was out of town, so her two children would have to come along with them. They, however, *didn't* see eye-to-eye with their mom's plans. They wanted to stay home—and were being anything but cooperative!

Suz is a wonderful mom who knows how to sidestep power struggles, and with some coaxing, can get her children on the same page while allowing them to feel they have kept their independence. That doesn't mean, however, that siblings won't decide to wage war in the back seat once on they are on their way there. She now had two screaming children strapped in car seats!

Remaining calm, and keeping her sense of humor and perspective, she offered distracting topics that took the focus off the battle and changed the situation into an unwitting surrender for the pair. *DISTRACTION*, it works almost every time. They headed into the restaurant.

Despite the difficult start to the evening, they ended up having a very enjoyable experience and stayed for about an hour and a half. Suzanne paid for their meal, and they made their way outside. As they walked back to the car, she pulled open her purse and started digging for her car keys.

The low outdoor light didn't help, and she started getting frustrated that she couldn't find them. *Did I leave them in the restaurant?* she wondered.

When they got to her car, she set her purse down on the hood of the car to start taking things out to find the keys. "Where are they?" She was very puzzled.

Just then, Suz noticed a strange vibration…

Her car was running! She peeked inside, and there in the ignition were her keys. The distraction worked all right—she'd left the car unlocked and running the entire time, they were in the restaurant!

#20 – CHEATERS, CHEATERS, EVERYWHERE

Lasik eye surgery was becoming more and more affordable. And when comparing the cost of the surgery versus the cost of glasses, lenses, contacts, contact solution, and eye drops, Joni saw that there would be a savings after the first year.

She used her flex account money, a work benefit, to have the surgery done in early October. It was one of the best things she'd ever done for herself. After only four hours of sleep and eye healing time, she peeked outside, and for the first time since fourth grade, could see the crisp fall colors and the details of the trees without glasses.

Wow, what an incredible feeling! she thought. While she didn't need to wear glasses and contacts anymore, she did need to have on hand those over-the-counter glasses, commonly called "cheaters," when reading fine print. This was a very small sacrifice.

She's known to lose not only numerous pairs of inexpensive sunglasses but her cheater glasses as well. Over time, to circumvent not being able to find a pair, she accumulated a small collection. She had a pair in her kitchen, one in her home office, one in the car, a magnifying lens on a bookshelf, which her sons *relentlessly* teased her about, and a pair at work.

As part of her job, she reviewed contract agreements and certificates of insurance. As you can imagine, the print is extremely small on these types of documents. Arms can't be held out far enough to read them unless you hand them to someone else to hold! While that's a funny way to read small print, it is impractical, and cheaters are a necessity.

Why can't the print be smaller on the bathroom scale, *or other things we* DON'T *want to see, instead of on work papers?* was Joni's thought.

A coworker brought her a contract to review, and for the life of her, she couldn't find her cheaters. They patted down the paperwork on her desk, lifted folders, moved papers, she checked her purse, and they looked on the floor. No glasses. She started to retrace her steps from earlier that morning.

She checked at the front desk, then went into the restroom to check the small counter that was to the right as you entered. She went to other coworkers' desks to see if she'd left them behind, but no cheaters turned up. Everyone was willing to help find her cheaters, but all searches ended up useless.

She then headed to the kitchen. A few people were in there getting coffee and mid-morning snacks, and she asked them if they had seen her cheaters. "What do they look like?" someone asked. "They have black on the front frame and wooden bamboo bows."

She then heard Jim ask, "Are you trying to find these?" She glanced up and watched him as he reached upward… and removed her cheaters from the top of her head. Not only had she *not* noticed they were on her head, but all the people helping her didn't see them either. She now carries a pair in her purse.

#21 – WHICH SIDE ARE YOU ON?

Daughters who have a tight bond with their mothers are sure to catch up with each other on a regular basis. Life happens so fast, and when so many things change daily, pausing for reflection and sharing is deeply gratifying—and fun!

Courtney is a creative and lively person. Her sparkling energy is just as infectious as her laugh, and she has one of these tight bonds with her mom.

They had planned to meet for lunch at a local sandwich shop. Courtney was not enthusiastic about going to this particular sandwich shop. She was trying to stick to a healthy eating plan, and while this certain eatery didn't have the healthiest choices, they had a few menu items that would do, so she agreed to meet there.

Knowing she'd another errand to run before returning to work, Courtney let her mom know that she'd have to cut their lunch a bit short. There was so much to talk about in a short amount of time.

She and her husband were amid building a home, and there were so many new details to share. John, her husband, was stationed overseas on another tour for the military, so she also brought her mom up to speed on the conversations with him.

The lunch hour sailed by, and before long, it was time to get going. She said goodbye to her mom and headed out to the parking lot.

When she got to the car, she opened the door and sat down. Taking a deep breath, she was running over in her mind the errand she'd left to do, and she sat there waiting to go. Eager to get the show on the road, but feeling that *something* was not quite right, she glanced around and realized…She was sitting in the passenger side of the car—even though *SHE* was the driver! In her hurry, she'd forgotten they had driven separate cars.

Bursting out with that infectious laugh, Courtney got out of the passenger's side of the car and made her way to sit where she belonged—the driver's side.

#22 – SEE YOU AT THE MOVIES!

Over the past couple of decades, book clubs have turned out to be very popular, for the most part, amongst women. Oprah had a very popular talk show that launched a book club with an enormous following. You could walk into your neighborhood bookstore, and close to the entry were books on display with a circular label that read, "Oprah's Book Club." The books flew off the shelves, and the authors became best sellers.

The momentum and exposure of that famous book club generated a resurgence of book clubs across the country. While some clubs are online, many of these clubs are in-person and vary in their focus.

A handful are strictly the serious study of the literary greats, while other clubs have found a balance of incorporating a wide variety of topics—including reading funny books that offer not only stimulating conversation but the ability to be silly and laugh about ourselves with a *LOT* of wine!

Kathy joined her neighborhood book club several years ago. This type of book club offered not only a convenient proximity, but created more meaningful connections with her neighbors.

One novel that they had previously read had been made into a popular movie. Anticipation built in the days before the movie's local release, and the group got together for a meeting. They discussed going to watch and see if the movie's portrayal did justice to the book's original story. It was decided that those interested would meet at the theatre at a particular date and time.

Kathy arrived a bit early. She purchased her ticket, bought some popcorn, and headed in to grab some seats. Not spotting anyone from her group, she decided that she was the first one to arrive.

She got comfortable in her seat, relaxing as she waited. The previews came and went. Now, this was pre-texting days, so she peeked at her watch, and continued to wait and wonder.

Where is everyone? Are they gathering in the lobby and waiting to come in together?

Then, the movie began, and Kathy had a sinking feeling that she was *NOT* the first attendee... She was sitting in the *wrong* movie theatre complex!

What's a girl to do?

She settled back into her seat and watched the epic love story all by herself!

#23 - HOLD WHAT?

A couple of months after successful breast surgery and radiation for breast cancer, Jean woke one morning, unable to get out of bed. She was having an immobilizing back spasm. *But, what if it isn't a spasm?*
What if I'm paralyzed?
What if I can't get to a phone?
What if nobody misses me for days?
Jean self-admittedly describes herself as tending to be a little bit dramatic. She didn't have a phone in her bedroom, so she gingerly crept, inch by inch, and an hour later made it to a phone.

She called her oldest daughter (apparently 911 wasn't dramatic enough). "Come *RIGHT AWAY,* and take me to the emergency room!" Something was terribly wrong, so she urged her daughter. "*Please* hurry!"

It took about forty minutes before her daughter arrived at the house, and by then, Jean could move better. Despite her improved mobility, they recognized that she still needed to be checked out.

At the emergency room, the doctor felt a few tests were in order, especially given the fact that she'd had surgery so recently. One of the tests was a scan not only of her back but also of her chest area.

Jean was helped onto the narrow table that was attached to the circular machine that appeared to resemble a giant plastic toilet paper roll.

The technician told her that the table would glide slowly into the machine. He told her that they needed her to remain very still during the scan. That she would hear some buzzing and popping noises, and when the test was complete, the table would slowly slide back out.

He told her that they would be in a little control booth behind her, watching to make sure she was doing okay, and that they would provide additional instructions to her on an overhead speaker.

With that, he disappeared out of sight.

Jean lay there, very still, arms at her sides, not moving, following directions, when a loud voice came over the speaker and said, "JEAN, *HOLD* YOUR BREAST."

Hold my breast?

But the voice had a very serious tone to it. She knew she was supposed to lay very still, but *perhaps* this request had something to do with the recent surgery of her right breast. *Maybe they needed it covered?*

His authoritative tone rang out like he meant business and that she needed to follow his directions. As to not move any other part of her body, she hesitantly, and very slowly, bent her right arm and began to rotate it counterclockwise at the elbow, moving it up toward her breast, palm down, inching it as *slowly* as she could.

Her hand hovered just over her breast when she thought, *this doesn't make any sense!* Just as her hand came to cup her right breast, the same authoritative voice came over the speaker.

"JEAN, RELEASE YOUR *BREATH.*" *Ohhhhh… breath,* not *breast!*

#24 – LET ME DRIVE!

Courtney and her husband had a new home under construction. Her husband was deployed overseas, leaving Courtney to coordinate their joint decisions with the builder. The process involved meeting the many subcontractors on site to approve work and materials.

Some of the shorter appointments she could take care of during lunch, but some required her to leave work early to meet after hours. Her sister wanted to get together with her on one of the nights. They had discussed possibly going out with friends that evening, and if they could arrange to meet halfway, then they could drive together.

They chose to meet at a gas station that had some extra commuter parking. Courtney's sister arrived shortly after she did. She got into her sister's car, and they headed to the construction site.

Courtney was meeting with a woman who would be installing some closet solutions in the home. Her sister had been living with her, so having her along for these decisions would be a big help and a fun way to spend time together.

They wanted to set up the closets in a way that would maximize any dead space, making them as efficient as possible. They were also going to determine where closet lighting would be needed. The meeting went quickly, and before long, Courtney and her sister were ready to leave.

She received a text from some friends asking for confirmation that she and her sister would be meeting them for dinner. "Sure!" she said. This was an opportunity for her to unwind and just enjoy a relaxing night without thinking about construction costs, deadlines, and unexpected changes.

They had a great time visiting with everyone over dinner. The whole group had early work schedules the next day, so goodbyes were said after a few hours, and the sisters made their way home.

The next morning, after Courtney finished getting ready for work, she settled her German Shepard, Felix, in for the morning. She would be back during lunch to check on him. Her sister had already left for work.

She grabbed her keys, opened her garage, and stepped into the garage.

Her car was *gone*! Thoughts were racing. *Did my car get stolen? This has not happened in this neighborhood.* She stood there flabbergasted.

Suddenly it hit her, a wave of realization...She'd *left* her car at the gas station the night before! With her sister already at work, Courtney called a coworker to pick her up and drive her to the gas station to get her car that had been sitting there since 5:00 p.m. the prior day.

#25 – IT'S PUMPING COLD OUT HERE!

On a bitterly cold winter evening in February, Rozie went downtown with her daughter. She'd purchased tickets for the Illusion Theatre through a silent auction, and this was the evening they had chosen to go and see a show.

The play finished about 10:00 p.m. As they drove out of the Macy's parking ramp, Rozie began sharing with her daughter a couple of milestones that had happened during her lunch that day.

She and her husband were in the midst of a divorce, and it was somewhat significant that today they had filed their taxes together for the very last time. No matter how long you have been married, divorce is a major change, and with it, certain milestones bring a quiet feeling of confidence.

Rozie had also been known to procrastinate filling her gas tank until it was absolutely necessary. But today, when she heard the weather was going to turn bitterly cold, and she knew she didn't want to be pumping gas in the frigid temperatures, she'd filled the car during lunch *before* the tank was empty. She prepaid for her gas so she could take advantage of a five cent per gallon coupon. Another feeling of accomplishment.

For some reason, her daughter glanced over at her and asked, "How much gas did you get?" Rozie peered down at her gas gauge, and to her horror, saw the needle pointed at "E". "OMG, I didn't get any gas!" She gasped as she gazed back up at her daughter. "I went in and paid for my gas and forgot to pump it!"

Her daughter started laughing hysterically and said her usual one-liner she uses when Rozie does things like this. "One step closer to the nursing home, Mom." Rozie burst out laughing. Her biggest fear was that she would be out the twenty-five bucks she'd already paid for the gas.

After she dropped her daughter off at her apartment, she stopped back at the Holiday gas station where she'd purchased gas earlier that day. She was feeling very foolish as she explained her story to the clerk. She was told that the clerk from earlier in the day had left a message for the evening staff that a woman had paid for her gas but had never pumped it.

"You aren't the only person who has paid for their gas and driven off without filling their tank!" the clerk said, smiling ear to ear. She wasn't sure if he was just being kind or if there really were others out there as flaky as she.

Despite her pro-active efforts, there she was, outside, shivering at about 10:30 p.m., pumping her gas in the bitter cold.

#26 – ONE HOT CART!

There are people who find pleasure in grocery shopping. They enjoy picking out produce: smelling, thumping, squeezing, and poking to pick the ones that are *just right*. And then there are the taste samples stations where you can taste a delicious new cheese or a wide variety of new products. Instead of a chore, for many, it is an experience.

Then you have those who just want to quickly cruise the aisles, get the basic essentials, and get the heck out of Dodge!

BJ fit into that second group.

One afternoon, she was out grocery shopping with her youngest son. She quickly made her way through the aisles and in true BJ form, with a firm flick of her wrist, roughly tossed each item she grabbed into the cart.

She wasn't in a hurry; this was just the way she did her shopping.

As they turned into the next aisle, out of the corner of her eye, she thought she saw a wisp of smoke in her cart.

She paused and thought, *I'm seeing things*, and continued shopping.

A few more minutes passed.

As she tossed another item into the cart she once again thought she saw smoke, this time a more distinct trail.

Oh, my gosh, what is going on? Was that smoke? Nah… couldn't be! With that, she kept on shopping.

She was searching the shelves for an item, and as she turned around, she saw a bigger billow of smoke.

"Oh, no, my cart is on fire!" she shouted to her son.

The smoke grew. She couldn't see any flames, but she didn't want to chance touching or moving anything in the cart.

She didn't have any water or coffee with her, but knew she needed to put out this fire!

The service counter, I'll go to the service counter, they can help me!

So, BJ, her cart billowing with smoke that now trailed behind her, made her way toward the service counter—and not with speed, but at a causal pace—*perhaps no one will notice if I walk at a normal pace!*

Her son was so mortified and embarrassed that he pretended he didn't know her and left the store to wait in the car.

And when she got to the service counter, *as if it wasn't already obvious*, she calmly said, "My cart is on fire. Do you have any water?"

One of the guys rushed to get a large cup of water and threw it on the smoking items.

As they sifted through the wet groceries to figure out what was smoking, they uncovered a smoldering box of wood stick matches. Apparently, BJ's firm wrist toss caused a few matches to rub together and ignite!

Embarrassment gave way to relief, and she had a good laugh with the guys who helped her, because, as BJ said, "Well, the whole thing was just kind of stupid!"

#27 – FIRE AND BRIMSTONE?

Mission trips to help build homes in struggling countries are a wonderful way for a group of like-minded people to get involved. Not only is a home for a family in need built in just one week, but you also meet new people and experience a new culture.

BJ and her son went to Guatemala on a mission trip to build a house. They had several days after the project was completed for sightseeing that included visiting some historic sites and some local churches.

There was one church that BJ was very excited to visit. The locals had shared with them its rich history, described its beauty, and as they drove closer, she could see just how stunning it was.

"Wow—it's *gorgeous*!" It took her breath away.

With the enthusiasm of a little kid, she ran right into the church.

As she was heading up the aisle toward the altar, she noticed that her right foot felt hot. Dismissing what she felt, she continued walking.

Once again, her foot felt hot. She lifted her foot up to peek at it, and not seeing anything unusual, she kept walking.

As BJ made her way to the front of the church, she could hear people in her group shouting. She couldn't make out what they were saying, so she turned around and saw them pointing.

Her eyes followed back down the aisle. Along the outside of each pew was a pile of pine needles, and in the middle of each pile of pine needles sat a lit candle. Searching farther down the aisle, she could see friends from her group moving frantically around a couple of these candles…a few others were pointing at her foot.

She glanced down at the top of her right foot and suddenly realized that on the top of her foot, in-between the sandal straps, was melted wax.

Looking up again at the commotion around the candles, she realized that she'd kicked a couple of the candles over.

In kicking over the candles, she'd started the pine needles on fire. The group she was with was able to put the fire out before it caused any damage to the church. It was a little smoky in the church, but everything was okay.

Everyone was laughing over what a funny clod she was, and her embarrassment quickly turned to laughter.

Her son was mortified, but that was not the first time.

BJ shared this and another story with a group of women who were sitting around a bonfire one night. She was sitting closer to the fire, making s'mores for the group, when it dawned on us. All of BJ's stories had to do with fire…

We all jokingly told BJ to "Back away from the fire!"

#28 - I WAS THERE

    Each year, Barb directs a community choir that performs upward of a dozen times during December. Somewhere between forty to fifty musicians travel throughout the area to churches and nursing homes, bringing the spirit of Christmas to the hearts of many.

    One Saturday evening, as they were planning to perform at a local senior housing complex, her mother-in-law, Jean, asked her to stop in and visit with one of her friends, Diana, a resident of the home where they would be performing. "Diana is a sweet lady and still sharp as a tack."

Whenever they sing at nursing homes, the house is generally packed. Residents invite family and friends, so the number of guests swell to fill the space provided. As the director, Barb's attention is taken up with the preparation, organization, and actual performance. It's not until they are finished that she glances to see who is in the audience.

Following the concert, she searched out her mother-in-law's friend, Diana, and not seeing her in the crowd, she asked at the nurse's station where she might find her. By this time, the woman had returned to her room.

Since Barb had only met her briefly once before, she explained to Diana who she was and how her mother-in-law, Jean, had asked her to stop in and say hello.

Then Barb said, "I directed the choir that just performed."

"Oh, yes," she said. "That was such a lovely concert." Then after a slight pause, she asked, "I was there, wasn't I?"

#29 – SAFE, SOUND AND SECURE

The home that Joni lived in had a horn mounted on the roof that remained from an old security system the prior owner had installed. The system no longer worked, but the horn on the roof had a panic button inside the utility closet in the kitchen. While she managed several times to send her neighbors jumping straight up in the air when she would accidentally hit the panic button, it didn't provide any security.

As her youngest son moved from the home, the idea of installing a new security system was the sensible thing to do. She had Miss Nala, her faithful dog companion, but now, living alone, the older home noises were amplified making sleeping soundly more difficult.

Joni's local cable company had a home security division, and they were running a special that included reduced installation and low monthly charges, so she called them for an estimate.

The wireless system was impressive with motion sensors that included two settings: "Arm and Stay" or "Arm and Away." The Arm and Stay feature is used if you are home and would like the security system on while you are sleeping. That setting allows you to get up and get a drink of water in the middle of the night without setting off the alarms and the police arriving to find you in your undies.

The cameras were accessible remotely, and you could see different rooms or the exterior of the home from any computer or Internet connection. Door sensors could be set with different tones so that if someone came in unannounced, you knew which door they accessed.

"Well, that's fun!" She wanted to add a little humor to the system, so she set the side garage door sensor to sound like a dog barking whenever it was opened.

This, of course, confused Miss Nala!

The smoke detectors and all other sensors were monitored, and if there were trouble, emergency services would be dispatched.

She felt she would be in safe hands, so she purchased the system and made arrangements for a service date.

The system was installed on a Saturday morning. Joni felt very comfortable after the technician taught her how to arm and disarm the system. She ran a few errands, and every time she would arm or disarm the system, her confidence grew.

That night she slept soundly, feeling very protected.

The next morning, her oldest son stopped over to go to the lake with her and Miss Nala.

He stood in the entry removing his shoes and asked, "So, how do you like your new security system?"

"I just love it!" she gushed. She went on to talk about all the features and how good she'd slept the night before knowing she was safe.

Her son chucked and said, "Well…you may want to remove these if you want to sleep even safer tonight."

And with that, he removed her house keys from outside the door!

#30 – SILENT RELIEF

Mary is a very kind-hearted, giving person—a gentle soul who is very involved with local charities and gives of her time until she's spinning in circles like a tightly wound clock. She has a very hard time saying *no* to anyone and ends up recruited for far more volunteer activities than her schedule allows.

It is characteristic of who she is, and it keeps her extremely busy.

One-day she'd to run to the grocery store to pick up snacks for an event later that night, and of course, she was in a hurry.

She rounded the end of one grocery aisle going at a pretty good clip!

As she entered the next aisle, she lost her focus and accidentally ran into the legs of a woman who was stopped directly in front of her.

Thud! The bottom rack of her cart hit the back of the woman's legs with pretty good force.

Before Mary could say anything, the woman whirled around and with venomous hatred began to spew out words that left Mary completely speechless!

This woman was up in Mary's face, wagging her pointer finger, screaming insults and curse words that just took her breath away.

Her thoughts were racing. *Is she going to hit me?*

Mary lifted her arms up in the air, waving her hands, trying desperately to get words to come out. She felt bad and wanted to apologize, but the anger pouring out of this woman left her speechless.

Her mouth hung open with her chin just about dropped to the ground.

But, no words came out. It was as if her voice was paralyzed with fear.

As she stood there, she lowered her arms and hands from the air, reaching to touch the side of her cheek with one hand and throat with the other. And still, no sound other than a little squeak emerged.

All of a sudden, the woman's face softened, and she gasped.

"Oh, my dear, I'm *soooo* sorry. I had no idea." The woman's face was flushed with sincerity.

She gently reached out and touched Mary's arm, and with her other hand pointed toward herself and appeared to be trying to attempt *sign language.* "Please forgive me. I'm so sorry!" She patted her chest with her hand.

Wait a minute, Mary thought, *this woman thinks I can't hear or speak.* Mary was still speechless, but she certainly didn't want to find the words to correct this woman so she could start shrieking at her all over again!

Mary remained silent as this woman continued to apologize. Nodding her head in a slow up and down *yes* gesture to the woman as they parted ways.

WHEW, she thought as she pushed her cart down the aisle. *I'm glad that is over!* Relieved that she would not see this woman again, she continued shopping.

As she rounded the next aisle, they met again, and the woman tried to gesture another apology.

"I'm just so very sorry, dear. I had no idea!" she said, her face searching for forgiveness.

And Mary, not knowing what to do, just sheepishly smiled, shrugged her shoulders, nodded, and continued on her way.

Not only did Mary continue to see this woman several more times in the store, but they also ended up next to each other at the checkout.

And Mary had to check out her groceries…in silence!

#31 - STATE FAIR LOCKOUT

Pat grew up in her state's capitol city, St. Paul, Minnesota, and so perhaps for that reason, she always loved the state fair. From the animal barns to the craft and produce displays, to the section of the fairgrounds known as Machinery Hill—she loved it all. For many years, her somewhat immoderate enthusiasm was abetted by her living no more than a couple of miles from the state fairgrounds. So, usually at the end of every summer, she'd attend at least one day and occasionally more than once.

The only obstacle in her path to pure state fair enjoyment was the fact that the university where she worked always scheduled the first day of fall semester the day after the end of the fair. Consequently, it was always extremely busy the weeks before school started, and sadly for Pat, coincided exactly with the state fair.

One year she was so busy—working well into the evenings and on the weekends—Pat thought she might not be able to get away even once. Fortunately, she managed to arrange a break from her work in time to cram in a couple of hours the last day of the fair. Her mind was full of all the sights and junk food-on-a-stick she absolutely had to squeeze in during the short time she had, so as she got to the fairgrounds parking lot, she was totally focused on finding a spot as close as possible to the first barn she wanted to see. Precious time passed as she hunted for an elusive open spot, and at last she found one fairly close to the horse barn. *Yay!* Time to get started. Scrambling out of the car, she locked the door and slammed it shut. In that moment, Pat realized she'd locked her keys in the car, her purse was there in plain sight on the front seat, and the car was still running!

What to do? Thinking back on it, she's realized she should have found someone in security who probably could've unlocked the car for her. But no, she appeared to be past all hope of clear thought. Instead, she hiked the two miles to her home for her spare keys. At least by the time she got back to the fair, her car was still there, still running, and her purse was still on the seat—but Pat was all out of time.

Disgusted and embarrassed, she drove back to work, and when asked how she'd liked the fair, she merely replied, "Oh, it was fine. Just as good as every year."

And she'd no doubt it was.

#32 - YOU'RE OUT OF HERE!

    Company sports teams are a great way for coworkers to bond outside the walls of their office, just hanging out with their team. The company Becky worked for had quite a few softball players, and they decided it would be fun to start a co-ed team. She hadn't played softball since middle school and never really considered herself to be a good player, but when asked to join the team she thought, *Sure, why not give it another try*, and she joined.

    The team consisted of twelve to thirteen players, a mix of employees and a few other people to give the team a decent size. They located a more laid-back, less competitive league in their area to join that played on Sundays—a day that seemed to work for everyone. With a team sponsor secured, they had their t-shirts made and were ready to play ball.

Some time into their season, on a Sunday afternoon midway through a game, the team took their turn out on the field, excited about their lead on the scoreboard. Becky was designated to the position of catcher and was feeling like she'd really hit her stride. In a rapid succession of pitches, the next player struck out. The inning was going very well for Becky's team, and as the next player stepped up to the plate, she thought, *I'm having so much fun. Okay, let's get another out!*

The first pitch was thrown, the batter swung, and the ump yelled, "SteeRIKE!" With the next pitch, the batter held his ground, and the ump yelled, "FOUL!" The count was at one and one. The next pitch flew over the plate and slammed into Becky's glove. "SteeRIKE!" yelled the ump. *Okay*, she thought, *one more strike—we can do this.* Another pitch came flying over the plate into Becky's glove. "SteeRIKE!"

Yes, yes, yes! she thought, and the rush of a possible victory was the only thing on her mind. She was so excited. They had just struck out another player. With that, she sprang up, and while pulling off her mask and kneepads, headed to the bench. She sat down next to one of her coworker's spouses who was keeping the books. Becky reached into her bag to pull out some lip balm, and as she applied the balm, the two of them talked about how great the game was going.

The field was full of excited voices, but Becky drowned out their sounds as she continued to talk about the game and glance at the stats in the book. The voices grew louder and louder, and suddenly, she thought she heard her name. "BECKY!" She gazed up. Her team, still out on the field, were shouting, waving their arms and motioning.

As she became refocused, she heard what they were saying. "BECKY, THAT WAS ONLY TWO OUTS! GET BACK OUT HERE!"

She sheepishly put her gear back on and headed back behind home plate.

#33 - WHAT DAY?

Dorothy loved going for leisurely drives with her family. They got an early morning start one autumn Saturday. The leaves were changing, and as they drove through the tree-lined roads, it felt as though they were driving through a kaleidoscope tunnel of brilliant color with a sapphire background.

The day was just warm enough to abandon sweaters and coats, but cool enough to remind them of the season change. They explored the back roads, where some followed along a river that wove its way through the fields and disappeared into the distance.

The noise of growling stomachs led the family to a local restaurant to enjoy not only a good lunch but also the delicious, fresh-in-season apple pie. Stomachs full, the family got back into the car to head home and enjoy the eye candy on the return drive.

As they came to a stop at an intersection, Dorothy noticed something that perplexed her. "Well, that's odd," she said. "Look at that strange sign!" She pointed to the passenger's side of the road to a marker that was across the intersection, which said "Day 2."

"Well, that's odd. Day 2 *of what?*" she asked.

Her family burst out laughing.

The sign was for the city of Day, population two!

#34 – WHAT'S *YOUR* FAVORITE?

Maureen loved the later part of spring. It meant her flower gardens were starting to bloom, and her vegetable garden had lots of tender plants springing out of the soil—it made for a great break after work to dig in the dirt. She loved to cook and bake, so the fresh produce to come meant that she and her family had many wonderful meals to look forward to.

She was very active in a local women's group that got together once a month to discuss a wide variety of subjects. In-between meetings they would take in a movie, go out on walks, or just get together for a potluck gathering.

On this Saturday afternoon, the group decided to meet at the gazebo at a local park. It was beautiful outside, and after their discussion, they planned to walk around the lake to get some exercise.

On this day, the topic was sharing things they loved. "Ohhhhh, this is going to be a great conversation," Maureen said to the woman sitting to her right.

What am I going to talk about? There are so many things! Her thoughts raced—how to choose?

One of her friends said she would go first, and she expressed her love of being a first-time, brand new grandmother. The joy of watching what a wonderful mother her daughter had turned out to be, that tiny bundle that she could spoil, and then send home with her parents...

Oh, that's a good one. I love that too! Maureen thought. She'd recently become a new grandmother and could relate to those feelings.

One by one, the women took turns sharing things they loved. Travel, their careers, reading, photography, scrapbooking...just so many things.

Suddenly, Maureen's bladder sent an urgent signal that she'd better find a bathroom soon! A nearby shelter had restrooms attached, so she quietly excused herself.

She tried to hurry because she didn't want to miss out on such a fun conversation.

When she rejoined the group, she heard one of the ladies say to her, "Maureen, Jan was sharing her favorite flour. Do you have one?"

At first, she was a bit puzzled by the question, *but*, she did *love* to bake and could share so much on this.

"Oh, my favorite flour is Gold Medal!" she said excitedly. "I've always used the same flour, well, except for that one time I had a coupon for that off-brand, but my cookies didn't turn out as well." And she continued, her hands animated in gesture. I'm not sure why, but I always get the best pie crust when I use that brand. I can't wait for the rhubarb to be ready!"

She continued rambling as thoughts raced through her head, "Oooo, and strawberry rhubarb is so good together too and…"

She stopped mid-sentence-noticing that the group of women were staring at her with mouths open and brows knit together in absolute bewilderment.

"Maureen, those sound delicious…" one of the women said. "But what is your favorite *flower*?"

#35 – GROCERIES, CHECK!

Kerry is a very organized person. Having meals planned for a week and a systematized shopping list is her modus operandi. Once her menu is planned around the various schedules and activities, she makes her grocery list and off to the store she goes.

Kerry bumped into a neighborhood friend as she returned to her car after one of these shopping trips. She unloaded her groceries into the trunk and put the extra bags in the front passenger's seat as they caught up on each other's lives. They had been trying to get together for a dance exercise class one night a week, but their schedules were hard to coordinate to make that happen.

They joked. "Aren't our busy lives like dancing? Maybe that is exercise enough!"

Arriving home, she unloaded the groceries and headed into the house. Her son met her in the kitchen to help her put away the provisions and share his high school day. There were so many busy and exciting things coming up: final tests, college letters coming in, and the fast approaching graduation party to plan.

The conversation was a welcome distraction as the last of the food was put away.

A couple of nights later, Kerry was looking for an ingredient for a chicken recipe she was going to make for dinner. *Where did I put those bread crumbs?* she wondered. She checked the pantry, and a few cupboards, but the breadcrumbs were nowhere to be found.

Quickly dismissing it as something she either didn't pick up or was misplaced when she put groceries away, she shifted gears to make a different chicken dinner. She went to get the teriyaki sauce, ginger, and green onions, but they too were missing.

What the…? I was sure I picked those up!

She knew she'd been distracted by the upcoming graduation and the overabundance of things to get done beforehand, but… *What's a gal to do?*

"We are having pizza tonight!" she shouted as she laughed off the numerous things she'd forgotten to buy at the store.

Later that evening, not finding her grocery list from a few days ago, Kerry tried to remember what she needed by going through her menu, the fridge, and the pantry. Her new list completed, she left for the store.

Her shopping finished, she headed to the car, and as she approached, she opened the trunk using the button on her key remote.

She reached into her cart, grabbed a few bags, and turned around to put them into the trunk.

And there, sat her missing groceries!

#36 – KNOCK THREE TIMES

Julie has a professional level position in a county government agency. With this position came a nice office that was not only quieter, but it also offered a place where you could have private, closed-door conversations.

One day she was meeting with a member of her staff for one of these closed-door meetings. The weighty subject being discussed needed further input, so Julie decided to bring in another supervisor to confer with. The other supervisor's office was down the hall, so Julie excused herself so she could ask her to join them.

She stood up and headed across her office to her door, and as she approached her door, stopped, and instead of reaching for the doorknob to open the door—she knocked—on her own door!

The employee sitting in her office burst out laughing. It was all Julie could do to regain her composure before leaving to get the other supervisor to come in and discuss this very serious thing that they were supposed to be discussing.

Julie was really hoping that was the end of it…but it wasn't.

At the time, the director she reported to was very solemn and stoic. Julie really liked working with her, but the director was always very serious. About a week after the knocking incident, the director came into Julie's office, closed the door, and sat down. She'd come in to discuss with her a serious issue the agency was having. It seemed that in this line of work there was always something very serious to talk about. When they finished flushing out some solutions to the issue at hand, the director stood up to leave.

As she approached Julie's door, she glanced back over her shoulder, gave her a half grin…. and knocked on the inside of her door!

Julie just about died.

This ended up being one of Julie's favorite, rare light moments that she shared with her boss. Her boss is now retired, but Julie is convinced that this stoic and serious woman recognized a White Chair Day when she heard one and found the humor in it!

#37- MINNESOTA NICE

Bonnie lived in Duluth on Lake Superior, one of the Great Lakes the Ojibwa call Gitche Gumee, meaning "be a great sea." This Minnesota port city is built on a gorgeous hillside that spills into parks along valley streams, eventually leading you to the lapping shores of this magnificent body of water.

Winters are full of snowshoeing, skiing, tubing—and the occasional *BIG* snow storm, making winter feel like "San Francisco on ice!"

As March drew near, it brought a storm that promised significant snowfall. Bonnie lived in a townhome complex and shared a home with another friend who was recently divorced. The garage held only one car, so the two women took turns, one week at a time, using the garage, while the other parked in the general parking spaces. As luck would have it, it was Bonnie's turn to park in that other area the night of a big storm.

Peering out the window, she watched as the snow fell fast and showed no sign of letting up. The winds were beginning to pick up, and soon the twenty inches of snow they anticipated was being blown and swirled everywhere, covering everything with large drifts, eventually making it impossible to see out the windows.

Resigned to the fact that tomorrow would be a "dig out" day, Bonnie settled down to an evening watching TV and a nice fire as a thick blanket of snow covered the city.

In the morning, her boss called to say that they were closing the office to make sure their employees were safe and staying off the plugged roads. Bonnie poured herself a cup of coffee, glanced out the window, and decided to eat some breakfast before heading out into the sea of sparkling white powder to dig out her car.

Bonnie started layering bundles of winter clothing, and as she looked in the entry mirror, laughed that she kind of resembled Randy, the little brother from *A Christmas Story* who couldn't put his arms down!

With a fleeting hint of blue sky, she trudged outside, shovel and broom in hand, headstrong and determined she would free her car.

After clearing a path on the driver's side, she used the broom to push the snow off the car's roof, exposing some of its white color. The distance between her car and the one next to hers was narrow, making it much more difficult as she cleared a path between them, working her way to the back of the car.

The bottom foot of snow was very wet, heavy, and compact. The top layer was lighter, a mixture of clumps and fluff that had either fallen or blown during the storm. She was sweaty, out of breath, but determined to get the job done.

When the blue sky would appear, the snow glistened an almost blinding brightness. Resting her hands and chin on the shovel handle, she paused to look around and catch her breath and mused how the parking lot looked like mounds of marshmallows, one after another, concealing the buried metal that lay below.

As she turned to the task of digging out the other side of her car, she heard a voice that was muffled by the layers of her knit cap, jacket hood, and the encircling scarf. Looking left and right with her limited vision, she didn't see anyone nearby, so she continued to shovel.

Again, she heard the voice, this time louder, followed by feeling something on the shoulder of her heavy jacket. She turned around to see an underdressed woman standing there with a pink nose and a *HUGE* smile on her face.

Bonnie pulled back her hood so she could hear.

"Thank you, SO much!" the wide-eyed woman gushed. "I flew in to visit my aunt and uncle a couple of days ago and was not looking forward to digging out my rental car. I've heard of Minnesota nice, but this was *VERY* nice of you!"

The stranger reached her arms out, embraced her, and a very confused Bonnie peered past this hugging woman's shoulder. Squinting to get a better view into the car's window, she realized…

…she'd been digging out *the wrong white car*!

#38 - THE SOUND OF CAPPUCCINO?

Marlene likes routine. She admittedly loves structured patterns, like eating the same lunch for weeks on end and having the same morning and evening customs. For her, *knowing* what comes next reduces the stress in her busy life.

One of her indulgent routines is to treat herself to her *favorite* coffee drink on her way home—an iced cocoa cappuccino. Taking that first sip after getting her drink at the drive-thru is a bit of heaven. The strong espresso flavor with its frothy foam is a welcome, cool, and velvety first gulp—the *perfect* cup.

She arrived home, shut the garage door, went inside, kicked off her shoes in the same old spot, and headed to the bedroom. Ahhhh—routine!

As is typical, she set her drink on the night stand and hurled her cell phone on to the bed so that after she changed, she could sit down, and check her personal emails while enjoying the last of her cappuccino. Marlene sat on the edge of her bed to slip off her socks, and the cell phone rang.

She reached her hand back to grab her cell phone, only to feel a wet spot.

Marlene had chucked her cappuccino onto the bed—instead of her cell phone!

So much for routine.

#39 - HOW OLD ARE YOU?

Not far from Nancy's home is a quaint little shop where she can pick up that perfect gift for someone *or* a treat for herself. New merchandise is always coming in fresh, and there is so much to examine—everything from jewelry to toys, clothing to accessories, and local artists' crafts to small house décor.

Nancy was having one of those days where she felt on top of the world. You know that feeling. The day is beautiful, and when you glance in the mirror you smile and think, *I look pretty good today!*

She grabbed her list, wrapped a fabulous scarf around

her neck, and headed out the door to visit that little shop before running other errands.

The shop is not only filled with unique treasures to hunt out—it *smells* exquisite! As the door shut behind her, she closed her eyes, breathed in the aroma, smiled, and opened her eyes to see a clerk smiling back at her. "Hello, how are you today?" she asked. Nancy shared with the clerk that she was having such a great day and couldn't wait to check out the new arrivals.

With no time commitments, she took her time strolling the aisles. Everything in this shop was a sensory experience, and as she touched, inhaled, and picked up just about everything, she managed to add a few things to her basket.

Success—some great gift finds!

Nancy made her way to the register, still light on her feet from having such a *feel-good* day.

Making small talk as she was checking out, the new lady behind the register commented on how good she looked. "Thanks," said Nancy.

Several times in her life she'd been guessed to be younger than she really is, and Nancy would attribute it to her plump cheeks that pushed out the wrinkles to make her appear younger, and laugh.

As she handed her credit card to the cashier, the cashier asked for her driver's license to verify she was the owner of the credit card. She glanced at the driver's license and peered up at Nancy and said, "I would have guessed we were the same age—you look so young!"

Without skipping a beat, Nancy said, "Thank you so much, I'm twenty years old." The cashier, eyes wide and speechless, handed her the bag and Nancy left the store.

Standing on the steps outside, it hit her. *Twenty years old?! I haven't been twenty in thirty-two years!*
Why in the world did I say that?
And a very young-feeling Nancy just smiled.

#40 NOT ALL ROADS

Nancy was going to meet a friend at a well-known local theatre along the river in downtown. Since it had been relocated to this new scenic area, a park along the river was added that not only allowed you to enjoy the river view, but it joined up with paths to a stone arch bridge. This old beautiful stone walkway stretched across the waters, and in the evening, offered breathtaking views of the city, its lights, and the waters beneath that danced with the illumination.

Inside there is access to an outside cantilevered bridge that juts out from the building toward the river. At the end of this seemingly endless bridge, you can purchase a nice glass of wine, go through a set of doors at the end to the outside seats. There you can gaze out, high above the river.

Nancy was so excited!

As she drove with her windows down on this beautiful night, she mused over the fun she and her friend were going to have.

Approaching the turn off for the venue, Nancy made a wrong turn and found herself heading toward the river bridge that would take her away from the city.

How am I going to get back? she thought.

She quickly made a right-hand turn and followed the road until she saw another, much smaller road, coming into view. She wasn't sure where it led, but she could see that it took her back in the direction of her destination.

As she entered this narrow road, she suddenly noticed that people were walking on both sides of her car, parting like a sea in front of her. Then, someone yelled out to her through her open window, "Hey lady! You're driving on the walking path!"

Shocked and embarrassed, not wanting to turn around, and trying not to make eye contact with anyone, she slowly continued driving.

The farther she drove down the walking path, the more she thought she could see in the distance that the path came out on the road near the theatre—*and it did.*

Once inside, she met up with her friend and shared her driving misadventure. They had a good laugh over it, then grabbed that nice glass of wine, (*Nancy could really use that glass right about now*), and they went to sit on the outdoor cantilevered bridge.

As they enjoyed the wine and the gorgeous view, someone sitting behind them said, "You should have *SEEN* this woman driving on the walking path tonight!"

With a gulp of wine still in her mouth, Nancy sputtered, and wine shot out as she burst into laughter.

And her friend? She mischievously turned to the group behind and said, "*Gee,* I wonder *WHO* she was!"

• • •

HAVE YOU HAD A WHITE CHAIR DAY?

We're looking for stories for
WHITE CHAIR DAY #2

Let me know at:

ihad@whitechairday.com

WhiteChairDay.com

THANK YOU!

Thank you for joining me in telling these humorous White Chair Days stories. If you liked the book and have a minute to spare, I'd appreciate a short comment on the page or site where you bought the book.

Reviews from readers like you make a huge difference to helping new readers find stories similar to *OMG! I'm Having a White Chair Day.*

- Amazon
- Barnes & Noble
- Goodreads
- iBooks

Thank you!

Joni Jesme

ABOUT THE AUTHOR

Joni Jesme is a mom, writer, and creative soul with wet feet, dirty hands, working on her 4th cup of coffee and continuously learning new things. She is employed in the creative world of marketing.

When sharing her first White Chair Day episode, she was surprised by the sharing of stories from others with their own similar, unique and humorous WCD moments. She gathered these moments to share in White Chair Days, the first collection of stories in a series.

Jesme lives in Minnesota and is working on a series of children's books with her sons, Aaron and Evan. A gardening and water-loving gal, you can find her wandering the woods with her sidekick, a Labrador named Miss Nala.

www.ingramcontent.com/pod-product-compliance
Lightning Source LLC
Chambersburg PA
CBHW071516080526
44588CB00011B/1452